A Republic of Virtue:

The Essays of John Quincy Adams

Edited with an Introduction by

Jeffery Tyler Syck

A Republic of Virtue:
The Essays of John Quincy Adams

Edited with an Introduction by

Jeffery Tyler Syck

political animal
PRESS
TORONTO · CHICAGO

Political Animal Press
www.politicalanimalpress.com

Distributed by the University of Toronto Press
www.utpdistribution.com

Cataloguing data available from Library and Archives Canada
ISBN: 9781895131758

Graphic on the title page: the Adams family crest. John Quincy Adams designed it himself when he had to present as an ambassador to a European court.

For my Mom and Dad - who have made everything possible.

Contents

"When virtue rules over the republic, what could be more glorious? Then the man who commands others is himself enslaved to no desires, when he himself embraces all things to which he educates and exhorts his citizens, and he imposes no laws on the populace which he does not himself obey but offers his own life as a law to his citizens."

–Cicero, The Republic, Book I

Introduction: A Statesman of Virtue

February 21, 1848, began like any other day for John Quincy Adams. He rose from bed early, had breakfast with his wife and family, and then left for the Capitol Building. Though weakened by a recent stroke, the aged congressmen still attended every meeting of the House of Representatives that he could manage. Adams' routine was interrupted later that day, however. In the middle of a vote, he collapsed. The House immediately adjourned, and the Senate and Supreme Court quickly followed suit as news of the elder statesmen's illness spread through the city. Several colleagues in the House carried him into the speaker of the house's chambers and in a matter of days, he died. 1

At the time of Adams' death, the country seemed close to splitting asunder, as the issue of slavery had torn apart any semblance of unity. But in the days that followed the death of John Quincy Adams, the country forgot these differences and united in grief. Every citizen of note within riding distance attended his state funeral in the city of Washington. Adams' old enemy John C. Calhoun joined with Henry Clay to help carry the congressman to his rest. Hundreds passed by his gilded coffin in the rotunda of the Capital. Senator Thomas Hart Benton of Missouri – a political and ideological opponent of Adams – spoke for the nation when he declared in the Halls of the Senate: "He [Adams] cultivated the minor as well as the greater virtues. Wherever his presence could give aid and countenance to what was useful and honorable to man, there he was ... Punctual to every duty, death found him at the post of duty; and where else could it have found him?"[1] 2

In the weeks that followed his demise, John Quincy Adams became even more popular and universally respected than he had been at any point in his long and storied career. The eulogies to his greatness published from all corners of the union made clear that this mourning went deeper than mere sadness over the death of a former president. America understood 3

1 Thomas Hart Benton, 'The Character of Mr. Adams,' February 23, 1848.

that Adams represented an idea already fading into distant memory - one for which they already felt small pangs of nostalgia. From Florida to Maine and everywhere in between, the American people understood they had just witnessed the death of the last and greatest defender of American republicanism.

4 Before entering the House of Representatives, Adams had one of the most distinguished careers in the history of the young nation. He previously served as a senator, ambassador to five major European courts, eight years as secretary of state, and a single term as president. Throughout this time, he earned a reputation for unflinching (and politically unhelpful) honesty. Driven by a strong mixture of Christian theology and classical philosophy, Adams saw it as his personal mission to help the young American republic come of age. In this respect, Adams' career was left unfulfilled. His own presidency was soon followed by the rough, demagogic, Andrew Jackson, whose hopes for America departed from Adams' institutionally conservative and intellectually broad-minded principles in almost every way. Adams' opposition to a new age of America hardened his reputation as an honorable opponent of slavery and majority tyranny.

5 His stand against the darkest aspects of the nineteenth century is what Adams is most famous for today. However, in his lifetime John Quincy Adams produced a steady stream of essays, poetry, and speeches that offered reflections on the deepest questions of political life. This literary output made Adams one of the most well-regarded thinkers and authors of his time. When Harvard University established its first chair in rhetoric, it was the young John Quincy Adams they turned to, and later in his life, he was made a member of the American Philosophical Association for his contributions to political theory. In his final years, Adams' efforts as a writer reached their philosophic peak as he re-wrote the social contract and outlined his own unique vision of America's philosophical foundations. Though well regarded in his lifetime, this series of essays and speeches have been almost entirely forgotten today. This book corrects that tragedy by reviving some of Adams' best works of political literature.

The Life and Times of John Quincy Adams

No human – no matter how remarkable or principled – exists divorced from the events of their life. In one way or another, we are all products of the people, places, and ideas we are exposed to throughout our existence. The life of Cicero is entirely confusing outside of the context of the chaos of late republican Rome, just as Alexis De Tocqueville's philosophy can only be fully understood with reference to his upbringing in post-revolutionary France. In this respect, John Quincy Adams is just like any of us, and if we want to fully understand his political thought it is vital we start by outlining his biography. 6

The Education of John Quincy Adams

John Quincy Adams was born on July 11, 1767, to John and Abigail Adams. 7
In a biography such as this one, intended primarily to provide a brief context to someone's political philosophy, the names of the parents are often mere factoids, but this is not the case with John Quincy Adams. As the oldest child of one of America's leading families, the young John Quincy was raised in the world of politics. Many of his earliest memories involved his father's political career and his mother's dedication to protecting her family from the battles of the American Revolution which, quite literally, raged around their home.

Though formally educated at many of the best schools in the world, 8
much of Adams' intellectual upbringing was in his parents' hands. Throughout Adams' life, his father peppered him with reading recommendations and demanded to receive full accounts of his son's reflections on current events and philosophy. Rarely did the senior Adams allow these commentaries to go unchallenged; he frequently critiqued his son's ideas and forced him into acerbic debates. Abigail Adams meanwhile served as the primary tutor to her children during their early childhood. Much of the content she covered consisted of the basics of reading and writing, but she also instructed her children in heavier subjects such as philosophy, literature, and religion. Given all of this, it is unsurprising that Adams' political thought was tinged with some of the dispositionally conservative federalism of his parents. Time and again, he showed himself distrustful of the

masses and vastly preferred the rigidly segmented institutions of the British and Roman governments to more rationalistic constitutional schemes. Though Adams also broke from his parents in important ways – adopting a more liberal and optimistic religious outlook that subtly altered his political trajectory away from that of his father's.

9 In the course of this education, Adams developed a particular fondness for the writers of classical antiquity – Tacitus, Polybius, Plato, and above all others Cicero. Early on, the Roman statesman and philosopher Marcus Tullius Cicero became something of a hero for Adams. A philosophic skeptic who nonetheless adopted a firm belief in the importance of virtue and duty, Cicero brought to Adams' puritanical upbringing a more organic approach to ethics.

10 At the age of ten, John Quincy Adams accompanied his father to Paris after the United States appointed the senior Adams ambassador to France. There John Quincy was enrolled in school where he was first exposed to the culture and philosophy of Europe, unfiltered through his parent's American perspective. Several years later, Adams' incredible skill with the French language landed him an appointment as secretary to the United States ambassador to Russia. This was the beginning of a long career in diplomatic service that more or less dominated the first half of Adams' life.

11 Adams' parents eventually cut his time in Europe short because they believed that prolonged education in the cradle of aristocracy might make their son too foreign and consequently functionally ineligible for a career in politics. This demonstrates that from the earliest days of John Quincy Adams' life, his parents bred him for one purpose – political greatness. Neither John nor Abigail where shy about sharing this information with their son and often reminded him of his duty to bring honor to the family name. Upon his return to the United States, Adams enrolled at Harvard University and soon after graduating, despite his lack of interest in the subject, trained to become a lawyer with a close associate of his father.

12 While at Harvard, John Quincy Adams underwent one of the spiritual transformations that redefine human lives. Though raised to aspire to virtue and human excellence, Adams' realized that he was in truth not a very good person. He aspired to do great things in this life – to change the world and lead his nation – but his motivation for acquiring power boiled down to simple vanity. Confronted with this startling fact, Adams decided that he had only one option – to seek all his life to improve himself. From this

point forward, Adams' diary – one of the treasures of American literature – became a detailed record of its author's never-ending quest for human perfection. This quest manifested itself in every facet of Adams' life. Over time he adopted a rigorous reading schedule and fitness regimen (most famously swimming in the Potomac River for a couple of hours each morning) to give himself a robust mind and body. Adams also constantly berated himself and others for moral lapses, not because he expected anyone to be consistently perfect but because he believed such reprimands were the only way to nudge oneself toward virtue.

John Quincy Adams newfound dedication to personal improvement 13 served as the culmination of his education. For the rest of his life, improvement would be his personal mantra – forming the core of his private affairs and his political projects. It is simply impossible to understand any aspect of Adams without appreciating the centrality of the concept of improvement in his life.

A World Beset by Storms

As Adams entered the legal profession, world politics began to turn on 14 its axis. Closest to home, the Articles of Confederation that served as the governing document of the newly minted United States quietly imploded and were soon replaced with the Constitution. Initially skeptical of the new government, Adams quickly fell in love with its careful dispersion of power and strong national authority. Soon after the ratification of the Constitution, the Electoral College selected Adams' father to serve as the first vice president of the United States – a clear elevation of the whole family in the social and political sphere of early America.

While the American republic stabilized into a true nation, the French 15 monarchy began to disintegrate. In the midst of an economic crisis and inspired by the American Declaration of Independence, the French aristocracy whipped up the support of the people to overthrow the regime and establish a new form of government. This set off a series of controversial and chaotic events that toppled the French monarchy. The French Revolution proved to be a thorny political issue in the United States. Thomas Jefferson saw the revolution as the next great step in the liberation of mankind, while Alexander Hamilton and John Adams believed it to be the prelude to tyranny. When England and France went to war, these more theoretical disagreements became more urgent. Jefferson pushed for America to firmly back France, while Hamilton lobbied on behalf of British interests. President Washington, understanding that this new country was not on a war footing with the great powers of Europe, ignored previous treaties signed with France and instead pursued a policy of strict diplomatic neutrality.

16 While these events unfolded, the young John Quincy Adams found himself saddled with a struggling legal practice. The failure of Adams' work stemmed not from ineptitude but from a deep disdain for the dry, rigid, nature of the law itself. He instead longed to take part in the thrilling political changes that surrounded him and yet, for now, lay just out of reach.

17 In 1792, Adams had his chance to break free and made his first foray into political philosophy. In a series of letters, he sought deftly to refute the arguments in Thomas Paine's recently published *The Rights of Man*. Taking a stance that blended the sensibilities of British conservative Edmund Burke and the liberal rights-oriented disposition of the American regime, Adams argued that Paine's focus on rights was worthy but far too abstract. Adams praised the British and American style of government – which he contrasted with that of revolutionary France – that he contended grounded rights in place and time and thus avoided the dangers of violent social upheaval. He also lambasted France's descent into raucous majority tyranny. Soon after, Adams published another series of letters that dealt more clearly with current events. Since the outbreak of war between France and England, the French ambassador to the United States Edmond-Charles Genet had sought to draw the United States into the war. As part of this endeavor, he spoke to large assemblies of American citizens – decrying Washington's neutrality policy and encouraging Americans to join the war effort privately if they could not convince their government to support their old ally. John Quincy Adams found such behavior by a foreign diplomat despicable and said so in a series of letters that defended the neutrality policy of the United States on both legal and prudential grounds.

18 Though Vice President Adams first showed disappointment at what he took to be his son's over eager intrusion into political debate, he soon became mollified by the praise that President George Washington heaped upon the younger Adams' literary endeavors. In fact, Washington was so impressed with the rhetorical skill of the younger Adams that he asked him to fulfill his father's old role as ambassador to the Netherlands. In this

capacity, Adams worked hard to maintain American neutrality in the war between France and England. It is also at this time that Adams met and fell in love with the British socialite Louisa Catherine Johnson. Over the protests of his parents, he married her and in time would have four children with her – three of which made it to adulthood. In quick succession, Adams served very briefly as ambassador to Portugal and after his father's own election to the presidency was made Ambassador to Prussia. Upon President John Adams' defeat in the presidential election of 1800, John Quincy Adams returned to the United States to pursue his legal practice and engage in political matters a bit closer to home.

Adams' second stint in Europe – when combined with his first – left 19
an indelible impact on his mind. Though he believed strongly in the superiority of American political institutions, it was in Europe that Adams first began to realize that America was so far behind its elder brethren in its knowledge of art and science. This deeply worried Adams for two reasons. First, he felt access to the liberal arts and scientific knowledge to be vital to human improvement. Without an appreciation for the world around us, he thought it impossible for humans to really be pulled from inside ourselves and learn to live lives of virtue. Second, he worried that by being culturally deficient America may reflect poorly upon the cause of republican government. Put simply, if the monarchies of Europe had a flourishing commitment to the arts and sciences, and republican America did not, Adams feared that this dearth of learning would be blamed on representative government.

Another by-product of Adams' time in Europe was the engagement of 20
his mind with the intricacies of diplomatic work and foreign policy. For the next several decades, these realms of public policy became the focus of Adams' political career. In his view, America could only enter an age of moral improvement if it could stand as an equal to the major powers of Europe. After his return to the United States, Adams was elected to the Senate with his first priority being the strengthening of the United States' power in the realm of international affairs. To that end, he promoted internal improvements (what we would today call improving infrastructure) and strict neutrality in the ongoing war between France and England.

Adams had been elected to the United States Senate as a member of 21
the Federalist Party. In the early years of his tenure, Adams voted fairly consistently with his party – pushing against the economic policies of the

Jefferson administration and promoting a robust national government. However, as time went on Adams began to break from his party on foreign policy, believing that many Federalists favored Britain to the point of obsequiousness. This independence from party would characterize Adams his entire life. Later in his career he happily declared that he had never affiliated with any party in his life. While only very loosely true, there can be no doubt that Adams never favored factional approaches to political debate and the initial sign of this neutral propensity is found in his Senate career.

22 The first glimpse of Adams' support for Jeffersonian foreign policy came when he pushed Congress to ratify Jefferson's purchase of the Louisiana Territory. Adams argued that territorial expansion would leave the United States better prepared to face her enemies. This break from his party ultimately proved forgivable but Adams' later support for the Non-Importation Act – an embargo that banned commerce with France and England – alarmed his commercial New England base of supporters. Even as the trade embargo proved both impossible to seriously enforce and a real plague upon Massachusetts merchants, Adams stuck with Jefferson and continued to fervently support the policy as the best way to keep the United States out of the war. As a result of these actions, the Federalist-dominated Massachusetts state legislature elected Adams' successor many months before the end of his term. Without the backing of his constituents, Adams resigned from the Senate.

23 John Quincy Adams' behavior in the Senate meant that the Federalist Party had no interest in putting him forward as a candidate in any election. Out of loyalty to his father, Adams also refused the offers of Jefferson's Democratic-Republicans to join their party. Instead, Adams focused on tending to his growing family and returned to his legal practice. However, soon after his election to the presidency, James Madison asked Adams if he would be interested in serving as ambassador to Russia. Though reluctant to affiliate with the Democratic-Republicans in the realm of domestic politics, Adams had to admit that he agreed with their foreign policy. In addition, a prestigious diplomatic posting would offer him a chance to rebuild his political career away from the partisan bickering of the United States. As such, Adams accepted the post and relocated his entire family to St. Petersburg.

24 Adams' time in Russia, though marred by the tragic death of a newborn daughter, proved a much-needed intellectual retreat following the

tragic ending of his Senate career. While in St. Petersburg, he befriended a number of prominent European intellectuals (including Czar Alexander I), began a lifetime practice of attending a variety of religious services to experience different spiritual viewpoints, and found time to read a wide array of novels and contemporary theology. This idyllic respite from politics was cut short when Madison asked him to journey to Ghent and serve as the lead American diplomat in the negotiations to end the War of 1812 then raging between England and the United States.

In the peace negotiations, Adams did his best to extract major concessions from the British, despite the United States' largely humiliating performance in the war. In the end, Adams managed to save face a bit, though the victory of the previously little-known frontier general Andrew Jackson did far more to boost American morale than Adams' diplomatic handiwork in Europe. However, Adams magical touch in foreign policy was quickly acknowledged by President Madison who appointed the still young Adams ambassador to England to try and heal the fragile relationship that existed between the two countries. 25

In England, Adams once again found diplomatic work to be conducive to an intellectual life. He and his family rented a small country estate just outside the city where he could study the stars and write poetry in peace. When in residence at the American embassy in London, Adams went for leisurely strolls with the philosopher Jeremey Bentham and they debated their often diametrically opposed views. As Madison's term as president drew to an end, Adams once again found himself – at his parent's urging – leaving behind his diplomatic work to return to the United States and throw his hat into the political arena. 26

This return to the United States proved to be incredibly well timed since it coincided exactly with James Monroe's election to the presidency. With Adams' unparalleled experience dealing with foreign nations, he was appointed secretary of state – a post that at this time was usually seen as a stepping stone to the presidency. For the first time since his ejection from the Senate, Adams' career seemed to again be moving toward his lifelong goal of sitting in the White House and leading his nation to its glorious future. Unlike some of his rivals, Adams wished to achieve the highest office in the country not through partisan maneuvering but through an impeccable record of policy accomplishments. As Washington entered the presidency 27 through his military achievements, Adams hoped to be propelled forward by his diplomatic victories.

28 Throughout his eight years as secretary of state, Adams' chief aim became to make America a strong independent nation. To this end, he pushed for the expansion of the United States into the West, engineered the acquisition of Florida, and drafted the Monroe Doctrine that sought to limit European involvement in the Western hemisphere of the globe. Adams' work in the Monroe administration represented the real capstone of his diplomatic career. For decades America had been a paper dingy adrift in a raging sea, Adams successfully worked to build a sturdier vessel so that his country could brave the storm of chaotic international politics. It would be wrong to say that at this moment America became a great power or that Adams alone can be credited with that achievement, but there is little doubt he did more than most in service to that goal. France may have had their scheming Talleyrand, England their clever Canning, but the United States had a principled Adams – for which we should all be thankful.

Triumph and Tragedy

29 In the century or so since he left office, the presidency of James Monroe has garnered a reputation for being an unusually tranquil one. Those eight years are most often called the Era of Good Feelings due to the persistent belief – based in public commentary at the time – that it represented the end of factional politics in America. Elected president almost unanimously, many Americans believed that James Monroe represented the death of parties and the return to a serene era of politics guided by calm consensus. Nobody bought this myth more than John Quincy Adams who sincerely hoped he would enter office as the first genuinely nonpartisan president since George Washington.

30 Why Adams believed this is a little harder to discern since he, more than most, was exposed to the dangerous tensions simmering beneath the surface of the Monroe presidency. For all the apparent calm on the surface, Monroe's governing coalition consisted of a writhing mass of petty feuds and court intrigue. Disagreements over slavery, regional resentments, and class animosities fueled a political climate of barely disguised hatred. All of this soon exploded into the election of 1824.

The election pitted Adams against three separate opponents – each representing different political factions and governing philosophies. The leading candidate by many reckonings was William Crawford. Crawford represented the hardline old school Jeffersonians who believed in a severely limited federal government and an agricultural republic. Henry Clay of Kentucky meanwhile spoke (along with Adams) for the modernized version of the Democratic-Republican Party that committed itself to serious economic development and a powerful national government. The wild card in the election was General Andrew Jackson whose victory at the Battle of New Orleans had transformed him into an American folk hero. At this stage in his career, Jackson lacked a firm policy portfolio, and support for him was driven largely by the recently enfranchised poor Americans who identified with his unpretentious origins and plebian style of politics. 31

Rather than serving as a steadying influence among the warring factions, the election of 1824 threw things into greater chaos when no clear victor emerged. Andrew Jackson won the popular vote but no candidate gained a majority in the electoral college. This tossed the election to the United States House of Representatives where a gridlocked Congress swung the election to Adams only after the Kentucky delegation suddenly switched their allegiance. Weeks later when Adams appointed Henry Clay, the powerful speaker of the house and a native Kentuckian, to be his secretary of state, he unleashed a storm of controversy. An enraged Jackson charged that Adams and Clay made a corrupt bargain to steal the presidency from the people, and a strong anti-Adams opposition began to form. The veracity of Jackson's claim that Adams and Clay struck some sort of bargain has proven difficult to judge. Though Clay visited Adams just before throwing his support behind him, Adams usually unvarnished diary says they only discussed policy. This seems entirely plausible – of all the contenders for the presidency, Adams and Clay were the most politically similar and it seems natural that such common ground would innocently bear fruit at some juncture. Yet, there is no denying that Henry Clay was one of the wiliest politicians of the era and every bit capable of ensuring that his loyalty would not go unrewarded. The truth is that we will never know exactly what happened and it matters little to discerning the reality of events that followed. 32

With a shocking mixture of nobility and naivety, Adams moved ahead as if he had been elected president by a wide margin that gave him a clear 33 mandate to transform his country. For most of his adult life Adams dreamed of leading his nation – of being the president who built upon the firm foundations of the Declaration of Independence and the Constitution a republic dedicated to the ceaseless pursuit of virtue. Overcome with joy, Adams could not conceive that anything might stand in his way. As such, when he spoke to Congress mere minutes after taking the oath of office, his speech struck a triumphant note. He declared that, "Standing at this point of time, looking back to that generation which has gone by and forward to that which is advancing, we may at once indulge in grateful exultation and in cheering hope."[2] He described in rapturous tones the success of every prior administration and announced America to be the most successful political experiment in history. As the address drew to a close, it became clear that Adams did not think the American experiment complete. With the passing away of the founding generation, he declared his own administration to be the beginning of a new age of improvement – a time to enshrine virtue in the nation as firmly as freedom or equality.

34 The language of the inaugural address was vague enough that Adams' opponents could not be certain of its full policy implications. Seven months later, Adams clarified his position when he sent his annual report on the state of the union to Congress. The report looked unlike anything the members of Congress had ever read, with an ambition far exceeding the proposals of any previous president. Adams called for the creation of two new executive departments, the founding of a national university, the creation of a national institute of science, and major infrastructure spending to economically tie the union together. He waived aside constitutional concerns on the premise that "the great object of the institution of civil government [assigned by the Constitution] is the improvement of the condition of those over whom it is established."[3] He also made clear just

2 John Quincy Adams, Inaugural Address. March 4, 1825.

3 John Quincy Adams to the assembled Congress of the United States, Annual Message on the State of the Union, December 6, 1825. This may seem a bit unusual for a man who once declared himself to belong to no party but the party of the Constitution. However, one must remember that both in our time and ours the idea of the Constitution as a strictly legal document whose meaning and application never changes has never been a universal view. Adams, following in the tradition of European thinkers such as Burke, took a more gradualist view to the Constitution. In his analysis, the Constitution was a set of norms and principles which held the government together and must never be broken. However, the exact legal statutes were of inferior importance.

how broadly he understood the term improvement declaring that "moral, political, intellectual improvement are the duties assigned by the Author of Our Existence to social no less than to individual man."[4]

Anybody but the unfailingly principled Adams could have foreseen 35
that such an agenda would face an uphill battle through Congress. The situation was exacerbated by the circumstances of Adams' election. Jackson's sincere belief that the election had been stolen from him – and worse from the American people – helped form the rallying point for an anti-Adams opposition to form. This collection of adversaries came to include such influential political figures as Vice President John C. Calhoun, former presidential hopeful William Crawford (who Adams inexplicably kept in his cabinet), and New Yorker political boss Martin Van Buren. This coalition of Western populists, Southern planters, and Northeastern merchants quickly ground Adams presidential agenda to a halt. The new Jacksonian faction successfully opposed the expansion of the cabinet, the founding of a national university, and the creation of scientific institutes. Through the sheer popularity of the policy, Adams managed to fund some major infrastructure projects – such as the one mentioned in Chapter 1 of this volume – but this was the limit of Adams' policy success as president.

Not content with simply killing Adams' legislative agenda, the Jack- 36
sonians started to organize a powerful political movement. Through the wily machinations of Martin Van Buren, locally influential men across the country began to affiliate with the Jacksonians. These men provided a sturdy web of supporters who could organize votes and local politicians to support Jackson and his cause. In time, this network of supporters would become America's oldest surviving political party when they started to refer to themselves as Democrats. The Jacksonians also began to buy and use newspapers to their advantage, viciously attacking Adams as too European and politically out of touch with his country of birth.

Though these clever political maneuvers were effectively ending Adams' 37
presidency before it could start, he could not bring himself to adopt similar methods in response. Despite the counter arguments of Henry Clay, John Quincy Adams believed that a president should remain above factional politics. What is more, Adams felt that Jackson's campaign methods represented an assault on the quiet, orderly, republic that had been carefully

4 John Quincy Adams to the assembled Congress of the United States, Annual Message on the State of the Union, December 6, 1825.

crafted by the American founders. By unleashing the fury of the masses, Jackson risked the destruction of a disinterested, dispassionate, government based on political consensus.

38 All of this culminated in Adams' crushing defeat at the hands of Andrew Jackson. This crippling political loss destroyed Adams. For the first time in decades, he started to lose faith in human improvement. How, he asked himself, could the United States have a glorious future if demagogic Caeserists could seize control of the ship of state? In the end, Adams rediscovered his commitment to moral improvement in re-reading the works of the Roman statesman Cicero, but he no longer took human progress for granted. The Adams that survived the election of 1828 proved to be far more politically savvy and philosophically realistic than the one that existed before it. Nonetheless, the guiding light of his politics remained the same.

The Last Great Struggle

39 When Adams left the presidency, he planned to follow in the footsteps of his predecessors and retire to his country home in Massachusetts. There he would spend his remaining years reading and writing political philosophy. However, these plans soon changed when several community leaders approached Adams to gauge his interest in representing his hometown in the House of Representatives. Feigning disinterest in the fashion of the eighteenth-century politicians he so admired, Adams replied he would do nothing to campaign for the position, but he would not decline if elected. Both his wife and son were outraged at the suggestion. They thought it undignified for a former president to return to office in such a lowly post and urged him to write back and decline the job before it was too late. Adams flatly refused, and on November 6, 1830, when his neighbors elected him to represent them in Congress, he recorded his palpable excitement in his diary. Adams' initial enthusiasm abated somewhat as the Jacksonian majority in Congress shunted him to a relatively minor committee chairmanship (manufacturing). Despite this setback, he resolved to relentlessly pursue the same policy of improvement that had guided his career since entering public service at age twenty-seven.

40 Adams proved far more successful as a member of Congress than as president. His first great chance came from the will of James Smithsonian.

Smithsonian, a wealthy Englishman, left the US government five hundred thousand dollars to "found at Washington, under the name of the Smithsonian Institute, an Establishment for the increase and diffusion of knowledge among men."[5] Many in Congress were inclined to refuse the bequest, given its strong British connection, or else to accept the money and use it for pork-barrel spending. John Quincy Adams disagreed and forcefully argued that this bequest provided a golden opportunity for the United States to lead the world in scientific research. In the end, Congress relented and appointed Adams chair of the Smithsonian Committee.

Almost instantly, Adams found himself besieged by requests from 41
schools and colleges for shares of the Smithsonian money. He quickly made the controversial decision to dedicate the bulk of the funds to create the national institution of science he had always dreamed of. He gave the general outline of his plan to President Van Buren before bringing it to the floor: "the establishment of an Astronomical observatory with a Salary for an Astronomer and Assistant – for nightly observations and periodical publication – Then annual courses of Lectures, upon the natural, moral, and political sciences – And above all no jobbing [patronage]."[6] Though many Jacksonians grumbled, Adams' cause won the day and he finally received his national scientific institute.

Adams also used his chairmanship of the Smithsonian Institute to 42
promote the construction of astronomical observatories across the country - awarding grants to the Navy Department, colleges, public school systems, and private societies for the construction of "lighthouses of the sky." Starting to understand the increasingly democratic character of the American regime, Adams set out on a tour of the West and North to promote science and lay the cornerstone of a new astronomical observatory in Cincinnati, where he delivered one of his most eloquent defenses of education, science, and the life of virtue more generally (included as Chapter 4 of this volume). This tour exposed many voters to the merits of Adams' scientific schemes and gave him a chance to deploy his rhetorical skills on behalf of an issue he passionately cared about. In short, Adams discovered at long last the power of shifting the sands of public opinion.

---

5 William J Rhees, ed., *Smithsonian Misc. Collections: Documents Relating to the Origins and History of the Smithsonian Institution* (Washington, DC: Smithsonian Institution 1880), 1-2.

6 June 24, 1848, in *The Diary of John Quincy Adams.*

43 Despite these efforts, it was not to education that Adams dedicated the fading years of his career – it was to the eradication of slavery. All his life, Adams had opposed the South's "peculiar institution." As a member of James Monroe's cabinet, he had been horrified by men like John C. Calhoun who embraced slavery and seemed willing to split apart the union to protect it. Nonetheless, Adams largely kept quiet on the issue until after his presidency. Foreseeing the great, glittering, potential of America that could lie ahead in the nineteenth century, he saw little reason to derail the future by stoking sectional divisions. By the time Adams took his seat in Congress, things had changed. First, he now occupied a safely anti-slavery seat that made opposing such bondage politically feasible. Second, his faith in progress had been shaken and he now knew that moral improvement needed a more forceful advocate.

44 Adams' fight against slavery never exploded into full blown abolitionism. Both for political and personal reasons, he consistently proved reluctant to openly affiliate with the controversial social movement. Yet his ultimate desire proved the same – the extinction of slavery in every quarter of the globe. To that end, he openly opposed the expansion of slavery into the territories. When it came to eradicating slavery where it already existed, Adams was more circumspect and deliberate. For one thing, he understood that the Constitution – as much as he may hate this about it - provided legal protection for slavery. Even more than this, Adams believed that the Constitution granted unofficial political sanction to slavery by ensuring Southern states were overrepresented in Congress.

45 Thus, in an uncharacteristically round about and prudent manner, Adams set about demolishing slavery. He initiated his assault by reading petitions from abolitionists on the floor of the House of Representatives. Predictably, this created a firestorm among the Southern delegation who quickly moved both to censure Adams and ban slavery from even being mentioned on the floor of the House. The censure motion soon floundered, but the ban on mentioning slavery – informally called the gag rule – persisted much longer. Throughout its life, Adams used the gag rule to expose time and time again the illiberal measures slavery forced Southerners to adopt not just against black people but whites. As Adams pointed out every time Southern delegates endeavored to "gag" him – if slavery could take away the first amendment rights of a sitting member of Congress, then who was really safe from its pernicious influence?

Adams' fiery tirades against the gag rule slowly spread through the newspapers of the nation to the American people. Many white Americans -whether they had previously approved of slavery or not – found that they agreed with the aged congressman from Massachusetts. As such, the tide of public opinion began to push firmly against the gag rule and it was eventually disbanded. While not an outright attack on slavery, Adams used this to weaken – though he was unable to destroy – the power of the slave interest in Congress. No matter how much they may have wished otherwise, Adams ensured that proponents of slavery would have to face their opponents head-on in the noble halls of Congress. 46

Outside of his work in Congress, Adams attacked the institution of slavery in one other way: his famous defense of the Mende people in the Amistad case. The court case centered around a group of Mende Africans who were captured in their homeland to be sold as slaves in Cuba. Midway across the Atlantic, the Mende revolted against their captors and took the ship by force. The United States Navy later captured the ship and the Mende people were put in United States custody while the courts decided their fate. The legal case proved an unusually complicated one. Various treaties with Spain seemed to give the young Queen Isabella II some legal claim on the slaves. In addition, the surviving crew of the ship argued that the slaves were their legal property, while the lawyers representing the Mende contended that they were being illegally held in the first place. After a series of dramatic and well-publicized lower court cases, the Supreme Court agreed to hear *United States v. The Amistad.* 47

Initially reluctant to be involved in the affair, John Quincy Adams agreed to serve as one of the leading defense attorneys in the case when it came before the Supreme Court. Adams finally agreed to serve as co-counsel for two reasons. First, after following the case in the papers he found himself increasingly invested in its outcome, but he also felt that his distinguished name would help lend credence to the claims of the Mende. On February 24, 1841, Adams made his four-and-a-half-hour defense of the captured Mende people. At the outset of his defense, Adams waded into the complicated regulations of 19th century international law – attempting to show that these laws rendered the Spanish claim irrelevant. 48

Concluding his more strictly legalistic arguments, Adams ended his defense on the grounds of natural rights. He declared that he took great consolation "from the thought this court is a court of JUSTICE. And in 49 saying so very trivial a thing, I should on any other occasion, perhaps, be unwarranted in asking the court to consider what justice is. Justice is … '*the constant and perpetual will to secure to everyone HIS OWN right.*"[7] He further argued that all humans are born with rights, and that these rights are not granted by governments based on the color of one's skin. The question then before the court was whether slaves were people. If so, then they must have rights. To prove the personhood of slaves, Adams turned to the Constitution, which he argued "nowhere recognizes them [slaves] as property. The words slave and slaves are studiously excluded from the Constitution … slaves, therefore, in the Constitution of the United States are recognized only as persons, enjoying rights and held to the performance of duties."[8] Given that the Mende were people and thus had inalienable rights granted by the creator of all beings, Adams did not see how the court could avoid siding with "the men who had resisted themselves to freedom, and secured their oppressors to abide the consequences of the acts of violence perpetrated against them."[9]

50 Ultimately, the Supreme Court sided with Adams. Though the ruling made it clear they found the technicalities of his legal argument more compelling than his appeal to natural right theory. Nonetheless, Adams struck one of the greatest blows against slavery of any individual until Abraham Lincoln ascended to the greatest office in the land.

51 In addition to his fight against slavery, the last chapter of Adams' life was also the period of his greatest philosophic output. Throughout his entire life, Adams was a prolific writer – producing travel books, pamphlets, and poetry at an immense speed. However, it was at this time that his writing became philosophic in the true sense of the word. Combining a lifetime's worth of reading and experience, he produced a series of lectures converted into essays that asked the fundamental questions of political theory. These essays make up the bulk of this volume and will be described at greater length later in the introduction.

52 An elder statesman with no more serious elections to win and nothing to lose is often the greatest politician of all. This is certainly true of John Quincy Adams. In his final years, he served as the conscience of the United

7 John Quincy Adams, Argument Before the Court, *US v. Amistad.* Emphasis in the original.

8 John Quincy Adams, Argument Before the Court, *US v. Amistad.*

9 John Quincy Adams, Argument Before the Court, *US v. Amistad.*

States House of Representatives – unrelenting and annoyingly principled. Because of this, his fellow members came to admire Adams. He may have been frustrating, maddening even, but they could not help but bask in the glow of his commitment to principle. By the time death struck its fatal blow on the chamber of the House, he had served his country, in some form or another, in every branch of government. He had been a writer and a poet. Most of all, he showed what a life dedicated to the service of his fellow man could be like. And it is a beautiful thing.

The Political Thought of John Quincy Adams

Perhaps because of his largely unsuccessful presidency, John Quincy Adams' 53
compelling political thought has been forgotten in our day. Remembered as the man who lost to Andrew Jackson and the son of a more famous father, he is rarely given the serious treatment he deserves. This attitude has left American political thought without the lessons of one of its greatest thinkers. Throughout his career, Adams proved himself to be a statesman and thinker deeply aware of the problems wrought by the Age of Enlightenment. More than any other figure in his lifetime, he fought to preserve morality in the face of scientific materialism and individualistic democracy. This is not to say that Adams merely stood athwart history and yelled stop. He believed that a serious opposition to the illnesses of modernity must have a positive vision of its own. His commitment to striving for virtue represents that vision. Adams understood that as difficult – perhaps impossible – as sustained human improvement might be, to give up would be to surrender to the worst angels of our nature.

Adams defined improvement in a very different way than many of us 54
today. To him, improvement meant striving for virtue – the ability to love others as much as one loved themselves. He believed that a human achieved virtue if they lived in accord with the fundamental teachings of Christianity: "That all mankind are of one blood, and the relation between them is that of brothers. That the rule of social intercourse between them is that each should do to all, as he would have done to him."[10] In short, Adams thought virtue to be selflessly living for others rather than oneself. Adams

10 John Quincy Adams, 'Introduction' of *The Memoir of The Rev. Elijah P Lovejoy; Who was murdered in defense of the liberty of the Press.* Pg. 6.

had no illusions that perfection is easy, or even possible. As he admitted, it is obviously true that the "human heart is deceitful above all things and desperately wicked."[11] But Adams also thought that "there is in man a spirit, and the inspiration of the almighty" that calls us to be better than our nature.[12] By this, he meant that every human has an obligation to work to rise above our selfish instincts, and by pursuing this impossible quest approach goodness. As he summarized in a letter to his son George: "as I know that it is my nature to be imperfect, so I know that it is my duty to aim at perfection."[13]

55 Unlike many moral philosophers and evangelical ministers in his day, Adams argued that only a rare individual can improve their nature without the assistance of society and government. This view derives from his total rejection of an individualistic state of nature. Following in the footsteps of earlier thinkers such as Aristotle, he contended that man is "by the law of nature's God, a social being. He cannot exist alone."[14] For Adams, man cannot live without society. Human beings need one another. He conceded that, "my character is (under the smiles of heaven) to be the work of my own hands," but those hands must be guided with the assistance of one's fellow man.[15] Otherwise, personal character inevitably descends into selfishness. Thus for Adams, the creation of a good government and society formed a vital part of the process by which humans can improve themselves.

56 Adams derived this perspective from his rejection of the Lockean vision of the social contract. Adams argued that families, rather than individuals, form the fundamental unit of civil society that comes together to form a government for the protection of their rights.[16] He thought that since man is a naturally social creature, the idea of him existing outside of the family is ridiculous. As Adams plainly declared: "The union of the sexes, founded in

11 May 6, 1827, in *The Diary of John Quincy Adams.*

12 May 6, 1827, in *The Diary of John Quincy Adams.*

13 John Quincy Adams to George Washington Adams, September 1811.

14 John Quincy Adams, *The Social Compact Exemplified in the Constitution of the Commonwealth of Massachusetts; With Remarks on the Theories of Divine Right of Hobbes and of Filmer, and the Counter Theories of Sidney, Locke, Montesquieu, and Rousseau Concerning the Origin and Nature of Government.* Knowles and Vose Printers, November 25, 1842.

15 May 16, 1792, in *The Diary of John Quincy.*

16 John Quincy Adams, *The Social Compact.*

the law of nature, necessarily precedes the social compact which constitutes the body politic, which is an association of families."[17]

Adams argued that this conception of the family as the fundamental 57
unit of society, when combined with religious morality, naturally leads to an emphasis on the importance of duty. This standpoint made impossible any conception of human beings without obligations to one another. Citizens must take care of their fellow men and treat others as they wished to be treated or risk the collapse of the liberal project.[18] However, Adams made clear that his emphasis on the duty citizens hold for one another transcends what is merely advantageous for the individual citizen or even the regime. Departing definitively from many of his Lockean contemporaries in this respect, he insisted that duty had little to do with self-interest and more to do with the obligations placed upon humanity by God in exchange for redemption.[19] David Greenstone has summarized the centrality of duty to Adams better than anyone: "Adams believed that human beings, rather than doing just as they pleased in pursuit of whatever preferences they happened to have must be controlled by their duties as well as their rights, and thus by the moral law to which any conscientious person would gladly submit."[20]

Just as the family formed the foundation of the regime, Adams also 58
thought that it served as a model for a properly arranged government. The purpose of a family is to take care of its members and to raise the children born into it to live a life of virtue.[21] This mission imposes certain limits upon the father–who Adams considered the head of any properly arranged family unit. He must tend to the needs of his wife and children and treat them justly.[22] Though the father has absolute power over his offspring, he also has a duty to treat them well. Adams argued that the government should function the same way. Father and legislator alike are bound by "the eternal and immutable laws of justice" and though "the violation of those laws is certainly within" their power, it is not within their rights.[23] From this, Adams argues that not all governments are legitimate: those that shirk

---

17 John Quincy Adams, *The Social Compact.*

18 John Quincy Adams, *Introduction of the Memoir of Elijah Lovejoy.*

19 John Quincy Adams to George Washington Adams, September 1811.

20 Greenstone, *The Lincoln Persuasion.* Pg. 200.

21 John Quincy Adams, *The Social Compact.*

22 John Quincy Adams, *The Social Compact.*

23 John Quincy Adams, *The Social Compact.*

the duties they have to their citizens also forfeit the love of their citizens. In such cases, citizens are obliged to work to reform the regime under which they live, and in the most extreme cases, overthrow the government which tyrannically rules them.

Virtue and Freedom

59 Adams' belief that the cultivation of virtue is the best response to human selfishness led him to develop his own conception of freedom. In Adams' early life, the definition of freedom embraced by most Americans undeniably emanated from the political thought of John Locke. Thomas Jefferson and his followers took as a given that man by nature had the ability to order his life as he wished. For them, this served as the basis of freedom and the essence of natural rights. The result was that man was freest when the government stepped aside and permitted him to live as he wished. Adams rejected this notion - he doubted that freedom meant living one's life as one wished. Instead, Adams argued that freedom is the ability to live one's life well. For this sort of freedom to be possible, individuals must be free of external tyranny (such as an overly oppressive government), but they must also cultivate self-restraint to free themselves from the tyranny of their own selfishness.

60 Throughout his career, Adams pointed to two recent events that he believed showed the nature of freedom and how society can work to free man from tyranny in all of its forms: the Protestant Reformation and the American Revolution. He argued that "[i]n the theories of the crown and the miter, man had no rights. Neither the *body* nor the *soul* of the individual was his own."[24] Though much more religiously open-minded than most Protestants at the time, Adams thought the Catholic Church–at least pre-reformation–had not allowed their parishioners to fully participate in the life of Christ. They could not read the scriptures in their native language, the sermons were usually in Latin, and priests existed on a social and intellectual plane far removed from their congregants. The Protestant Reformation changed all of this. The Reformation not only shattered the power of ecclesiastical authority, but it brought religion to the commoners

---

24 John Quincy Adams, 'An Address Celebrating the Declaration of Independence,' July 4, 1821. Emphasis added.

through the rise of religious education. As Adams once stated at a crowded Fourth of July celebration: "The religious reformation was an improvement in the science of the mind; an improvement in the intercourse of man with his creator, and in his acquaintance with himself. It was an advance in the knowledge of his duties and his rights."[25] Without the interference of the Catholic Church, citizens became intellectually freer. They could finally pursue virtue without having it dictated to them.

For all the great work done by the Protestant Reformation, Adams 61
contended that a vestige of political tyranny lingered over the Western world in the form of absolute monarchy. The American Revolution played a unique role in finally bringing forth a government capable of cultivating and sustaining freedom in its fullest sense. In his account of the road to American independence, the colonists had happily lived for decades with the same rights and privileges enjoyed by Englishmen in the mother country. However, after the French and Indian War, Parliament began to assert its absolute authority. It became clear to the colonists that "English liberties had failed them," and so in their fight against the "omnipotence of Parliament the colonists appealed to the rights of man and the omnipotence of God."[26] Thus Adams contends the prize of the conflict became "the liberty and the immortal soul of man."[27]

From this account of history, Adams argued that, in the last several 62
centuries, events in Europe conspired to make possible – though perhaps not likely - the liberation of mankind. In Adams' mind, the Protestant Reformation freed the mind so virtue could self-consciously be cultivated in the human heart, and the American Revolution set in motion the liberation of man from political oppression. This understanding makes clear that, for Adams, virtue and freedom are deeply connected. He boldly declared that there is an inseparable link between "knowledge, and virtue and liberty."[28] The three must exist together or they will not exist at all.

---

25 John Quincy Adams, 'An Address Celebrating the Declaration of Independence,' July 4, 1821.

26 John Quincy Adams, 'The Jubilee of the Constitution,' Delivered in New York, April 30, 1839.

27 John Quincy Adams, 'Letter Read at the Celebration of West Indian Emancipation in Bangor Maine,' July 4, 1843.

28 John Quincy Adams, 'Discourse on Education,' October 24, 1839. Emphasis added.

Virtue and Freedom

63 In a Fourth of July speech delivered in his last year as president, Adams articulated his vision of the Constitution with more clarity than at any other point in his career. He argued that the Constitution of the United States had three stages until it would be complete. The first was the separation of England and the formation of a regime dedicated to natural rights whose spirit was best captured in the Declaration of Independence. The second great moment was uniting the various states under one national government and constitution which brought order to the otherwise chaotic principle of self-government.

64 These first two steps accomplished; Adams argued that it was time to look forward to the third stage of America's constitutional development. He declared that Americans must work to "adapt the powers, physical, moral, and intellectual, of this whole union, to the improvement of its own condition: of its moral and political condition."[29] In short, he argued that the Constitution had established the primacy of natural rights and created the institutions that would protect those rights, but it now must work to improve the moral and economic security of the nation. This goal was important in part because it would lead to prosperity but also because Adams doubted a republic could survive without a virtuous population. As such, he thought it time to establish virtue as the heart of the constitutional order.

65 This goal served as Adams' chief guide to public policy throughout his career, but this did not mean that his life's ambition could never be threatened. No threat loomed larger in Adams' early career than mass democracy. In the specter of Jacksonian democracy, Adams thought he saw the Athenian mob – ready to unleash a tide of selfless cruelty upon his neatly ordered constitutional republic. As he put in his diary while a young man: "It is a very general political maxim, that Men can never possess a great degree of Power without abusing it … But of all Tyrannies, the most dreadful, is that of an whole people."[30] Consequently, Adams became one of the strongest early nineteenth-century opponents of democracy.

66 In his total dread of democracy, Adams followed in the footsteps of

---

29 John Quincy Adams, 'Speech at the Groundbreaking of the Chesapeake and Ohio Canal,' July 4, 1828.

30 September 28, 1786, in *The Diary of John Quincy Adams.*

most prominent republican theorists, who generally view the unrestrained will of the people as a threat to harmonious governance. It is for this reason, that throughout his long career Adams' rarely referred to the United States as a democracy. To his mind, the United States remained always a republic or mixed regime. He described this arrangement in his essay on the social contract: "It [the American regime] is not Democracy, - nor Aristocracy, nor Monarchy, but a compound of them all, of which Democracy is the oxygen or vital air, too pure in itself for human respiration, but which, in the union with other elements equally destructive in themselves and less pure, forms the moral and political atmospheric air, in which we live and move and have our being."[31] In short, Adams viewed the people as merely a part of the regime rather than the regime in total.

Adams believed that democracy sets citizens adrift from any chance of 67
human improvement. He argued that virtue is only possible through institutions that teach us to restrain our selfish passions. Democracy instead empowers each individual to rule without reference to anyone else. The inevitable result is that instead of empowering the populace, democracy makes them slaves to their impulses, "altogether incapable of forming rational judgment, either upon the principles or the motives of their own conduct."[32] In such a system, Adams did not think the voters could even be considered "free agents" worthy of blame or admiration.[33] They were merely pawns to be used by unscrupulous politicians willing to play to their passions.[34]

Adams' rejected such a system in part because of what it does to the 68
soul of the citizenry, but also because it leads to a political climate destructive of any pursuit of the common good. The rule of a mob managed by demagogues "can be brought to act in concert upon no other principles than those of frantic enthusiasm and ungovernable fury."[35] Such a system

31 John Quincy Adams, *The Social Compact.* In fact, Adams even went so far as to argue in his diary that Hamilton's proposed outline of a constitution at the constitutional convention was superior to the one we had ended up even if it was impracticable to implement in the United States. Among other things, Hamilton's plan had called for life tenure for presidents, governors, and senators. All of whom had been elected by specially convened electoral colleges rather than the people.

32 John Quincy Adams, *Letters From Publicola 5.*

33 John Quincy Adams, *Letters from Publicola 5.*

34 John Quincy Adams, *Letters from Publicola 5.*

35 John Quincy Adams, *Letters from Publicola 5.*

could create nothing of value to civilization, for all of its power "consists in destruction" for whatever meets the displeasure of the mob must be "devoted to ruin."[36] Adams summarized what he viewed as the tragic circumstances of democracy in his diary: ""Democracy has no forefathers – It looks to no posterity – It is swallowed up in the present, and thinks of nothing but itself – This is the vice of Democracy, and it is incurable - Democracy has no monuments – It strikes no Medals – It bears the head of no man upon a Coin – Its very essence is Iconoclastic."[37]

Virtue and Freedom

69 As time wore on, John Quincy Adams began to see slavery, rather than democracy, as the chief threat to human improvement. He firmly believed that a virtuous republic could not long survive with the poison of slavery running through its veins. Adams had not always felt so strongly about slavery. When appointed secretary of state in 1817, he had a spotty record with the issue. Like his father before him, everyone knew that Adams opposed the peculiar institution. However, this opposition rarely translated into action or tangible policy proposals. In fact, as ambassador to Great Britain, Adams unsuccessfully worked to return slaves captured by the British in the War of 1812 to their "rightful owners" in the states. However, in the eight years he served as the nation's chief diplomat, Adams' anti-slavery views hardened, and he started to view chattel slavery as the single greatest threat to the American republic.

70 The reason Adams shifted his views had little to do with his own political thought – at no point in his life did he think slavery anything but a repugnant attack on human virtue – but instead with the changing mores of the American South. In his early career, Adams felt the South was duly ashamed of holding half its population in bondage to the other half. While the South felt this shame, Adams felt that the extinction of slavery could not be far off. However, by the time he became secretary of state, most of the Southern upper class embraced slavery as a positive good for everyone involved in the enterprise. Figures such as John C. Calhoun happily declared that the principles of natural right "were just and noble" but they

36 John Quincy Adams, *Letters from Publicola 5.*

37 December 5, 1831, in *The Diary of John Quincy Adams.*

only applied to white men and that without the institution of slavery there could be no meaningful equality among whites. Such arguments were made possible by the rising intellectual consensus in the American South that black people were a different species of human altogether. A species viewed not much higher than the average farm animal.

Adam's argued that such racist rhetoric and "scientific" evidence derived more from human selfishness and bigotry than it did reason. In his view, black people are clearly every bit as human as anyone else. Such a stance made slavery indefensible on any grounds for, "The soul of one man cannot by human law be made the property of another."[38] Adams believed it logically followed that to dominate and assert ownership over another human thus violated the laws of God which supersede the laws and wishes of man. Because of the evil nature of slavery, Adams contended that every statesman must dedicate their efforts against the vile institution. As he summarized in a poem written in memory of his father: "Who but shall learn that Freedom is the prize; Man still is bound to rescue or maintain; That Natures God commands the slave to rise; And on the oppressor's head to break his chain; Roll, years of promise, rapidly round; Till not a Slave shall on this earth be found."[39] 71

In Adams' eyes, the way in which slavery corrupted the virtue of the slaveholders served as one of its greatest threats. He declared that "It is among the evils of Slavery that it taints the very sources of moral principle – It establishes false estimates of virtue and vice; for what can be more false and heartless than this doctrine which makes the first and holiest rights of humanity to depend upon the color of skin."[40] In so doing, slavery undermined reason itself, for to believe something so bald-facedly untrue, Adams argued, the advocates of slavery must abandon common sense in favor of mere prejudice. He also argued that "The domineering Spirit, naturally springs from the institution of Slavery," thus pumping a wave of tyrannical and illiberal sentiments into certain quarters of the American Republic. Such issues corrupted public leaders who could otherwise be of service to their country – men such as John C. Calhoun and Andrew Jackson. 72

Slavery also inevitably corrupted the slave. By denying them freedom 73

38 John Quincy Adams, 'Letter to A Celebration of West Indian Emancipation in Bangor Maine.' July 4, 1843.

39 October 30, 1826, in *The Diary of John Quincy Adams.*

40 March 3, 1820, in *The Diary of John Quincy Adams.*

and education, slaveholders also denied many Black Americans the ability to pursue man's highest calling – the attainment of virtue. Adams described the condition of the average slave in vivid terms:

> "Cursed by the mere color of their skin – already doomed by their complexion to drudge in the lowest offices of society, excluded by their color from all the refined enjoyments of life, accessible to others, excluded from the benefits of a liberal education; from the bed, from the table, and from all other social comforts of domestic life."[41]

Such conditions made learning and human improvement impossible. Like Cicero, Adams tended to think that without education and virtue, one is not fully human. For "limited as it was, reason elevated man above brute creation; and coupled to a disciplined will, allowed him to improve his condition in this life and prepare for the next."[42] Thus in his way he agreed with the slaveholders. Black slaves were not fully human, but Adams saw this as a tragedy. A consequence of their circumstances rather than inherent genetic differences. He thought it the duty of any good Christian to raise up people found in this pitiable condition, to give them the means to pursue virtue and fully attain their humanity.

74 Adams' greatest concern with slavery consistently remained its corruption of the United States Constitution. Adams argued that the Declaration of Independence served as the cornerstone of the Constitution. All constitutional interpretation must first contend with the inalienable rights declared in that hallowed document. Adams conceded that when framing the Constitution, slavery had been legally permitted in several articles, but he also contended that the principle of the Constitution – that all men are created equal – remained inherently anti-slavery. As he fumed in his diary: "The Declaration of Independence not only asserts the natural equality of all men, and their unalienable right to Liberty; but that the only *just* powers of government are derived from the consent of the governed. A power for

41 November 29, 1820, in *The Diary of John Quincy Adams.*

42 Tucker, 'John Quincy Adams On Principle and Practice.' History of American Political Thought, Editors Jeffery Sikkenga and Bryan Paul Frost. Lexington Books, 2019. Pg 273.

one part of the people to make slaves of the other can never be derived from consent and is therefore not a just power."[43]

Adams thought this contradiction in the Constitution – that its funda- 75
mental principles opposed slavery while provisions of the document itself protected the peculiar institution – created an unstable political order in the United States. In essence, it created a constitution at war with itself. Adams could not conceive how a regime so constituted could long survive. By the time of his tenure as secretary of state, he concluded that the bargain the framers made with the slaveholding interest of the South had proven itself to be a mistake. The compromise had been struck to ensure the survival of the union, but Adams doubted that the union could last much longer if divided between the slave interest and the free North.

The fight against slavery was the last great cause of John Quincy 76
Adams' career. In many respects, he lost his life trying to end the expansion of slavery with an eye to its ultimate extinction. This fight inspired Abraham Lincoln – who was serving in Congress the day Adams was struck down and who later completed the New Englander's noble quest. Yet for Adams, the battle against slavery did not stand alone. It was one cause among many in his effort to make gentle the savage heart of man – perhaps the noblest political effort of all.

Why Read John Quincy Adams?

The essays that are contained in this book represent some of John Quincy 77
Adams' deepest reflections on the questions of political life. They are arranged chronologically and contain topics as diverse as the evils of slavery and the virtues of astronomy. With the exception of the first chapter, they were all written in the last decades of Adams' life and though originally delivered as speeches they were later published as essays or book chapters for wider public consumption. Uniting them all is Adams' perpetual quest for human improvement.

Though understanding the theme of Adams' life and writing does not 78
necessarily make reading him easy. Adams is not an essayist in the sense of Montaigne or Isiah Berlin – he does not advance a clear thesis in a short, pithy bit of writing. Nor does he produce anything like the complicated

43 March 3, 1820, in *The Diary of John Quincy Adams.*

dialogues of Plato or the heartbreakingly elegant discourses of Rousseau. Instead, Adams most often advances his arguments through history. Rather than explore ideas in the abstract, he prefers to show how concepts have evolved over time and in the process awaken his readers to certain ways of thinking.

79 The two best examples of Adams' use of history in the following pages are his essays on education and the social compact. In both cases, Adams could have simply defined the term he was examining and then made a case for how society should function given this information. But this is not what he does, Adams instead prefers to offer a detailed history of education and the social compact. In his historical analysis, Adams tends to rely on the history of New England and its Calvinist forbears across Europe – his essays are littered with references to Martin Luther, the Protestant Reformation, and the English common law tradition.

80 There are two reasons Adams' use of history is particularly interesting. The first is it reveals Adams' general distrust of ideological thought experiments. This preference for grounded politics dates back to Adams' Puritan upbringing. In his "Letters From Publicola," he expressed his unyielding affection for the gradual march of liberal ideas in England and his undying detestation of the abstract, revolutionary, spirit of post-monarchical France. This is not to remotely imply that Adams disliked human rights or was a political reactionary. Instead, Adams merely displayed a lifelong discomfort with frequently discussing rights in the abstract and thus placing them outside of their historical and cultural context. To put all this another way, though Adams was one of the early republic's greatest proponents of natural rights and freedom, and though he grounded those ideals in the will of God, he found the safest practical foundation of our government to be in history. In his mind, human improvement must start with the reality of what has been and go from there.

81 The second interesting point about Adams' use of historical narratives has a great deal more to do with us – the reader – and what we can find in them. Compared to most nations, the United States is quite young. Our founding myths date back to 1776 and are not so much myths as cold hard facts that we can read, debate, and pick apart. We have no King Alfred, no Lycurgus, and no Aeneas. Our origin is well known. One happy fact of this is that the United States has a better chance of understanding its true

political foundation and thus building a vibrant regime on sure footing as time goes by.

The disadvantage of our national youth lay in the fact that our history is short and the ideas we Americans defend can be hard to anchor in a mythic past. As a consequence of this, Americans are inclined to base our political appeals on purely theoretical concepts – when we push to expand rights or defend democracy we too often describe those things in the abstract rather than as a product of our historical tradition. The problem with such unmoored political debate is that it often degenerates into a simple shouting match between different ways of looking at the world. The anger and bitter politics of ideology can quickly and easily descend into political gridlock at best and dangerously factional politics at worst. To put all of this more simply, as a new nation founded on universal principles, we can sometimes lack context for our politics. Too often in the United States political movements prefer to ground themselves on dangerous or strange abstractions that risk unsettling the delicate balance of liberal democratic government. 82

Adams' use of history serves as a corrective to the often overly ideological tendency of politics. He provides an alternative way of thinking about America – one every bit as dedicated to natural rights, freedom, and moral improvement as standard modern liberalism but without the baggage of rootless ideology.[44] In this respect, John Quincy Adams is America's Edmund Burke. By this, I do not mean that he is the founder of the American conservative movement, but something far deeper. Adams artfully takes the principles of the American regime and puts them in *context*. He is still very clearly American and he does not abandon the universal nature of the Declaration of Independence's principles – as his fight against slavery proves – but he in general grounded America in a tradition we can to this day still understand and use. To say that Adams is America's Burke is to say he understood and articulated the unique cultural tradition that is America – our ideas, our hopes, and our history – better than any other thinker. This alone is reason enough to read John Quincy Adams. 83

Yet this is perhaps not the greatest reason you should read John Quincy Adams. The twentieth century philosopher Leo Strauss once said: "We have no higher duty, and no more pressing duty, than to remind ourselves 84

44 1. Jeffery Tyler Syck, "Toward A Conservative Liberalism: John Quincy Adams, Slavery, and the Meaning of Freedom," *Pietas* 2, no. 2 (Fall 2023).

and our students, of political greatness, human greatness, of the peaks of human excellence. For we are supposed to train ourselves and others in seeing things as they are, and this means above all in seeing their greatness and their misery, their excellence and their vileness, their nobility and their triumphs, and therefore never to mistake mediocrity, however brilliant, for true greatness."[45] John Quincy Adams represents one such peak of human splendor. As a young man, he decided to dedicate his life to moral improvement. He spent the rest of his years on this earth fighting tirelessly for a better world. No matter the political ramifications, he always pursued the path he believed most likely to create the conditions for greater human virtue. Though he may not always have been right, the effort was noble and ceaseless. A life like that is worth aspiring towards. A man like that is worth reading.

---

45 Leo Strauss, 'Spontaneous Remarks on the Death of Sir Winston Churchill,' January 25, 1965.

Chapter 1: Address on the Fourth of July, 1828 (1828)

The first essay of this volume is not an essay at all but rather a short speech delivered on the Fourth of July at the groundbreaking ceremony of the Chesapeake and Ohio Canal. This particular speech has been included along with Adams' philosophic essays because he himself estimated it to be one of the very best summaries of his political philosophy. As such, there is no better introduction to the ideas of John Quincy Adams and his hopes for America. Addressed to a large audience of reporters and local citizens, the speech also represents the high-water mark of Adams' largely unsuccessful presidency – the groundbreaking of one of a handful of infrastructure projects that he managed to shepherd through Congress. Though the C&O Canal closed in 1924, Adams' soaring rhetoric captures much of the hope a younger generation once felt for America's future.

Friends and fellow citizens: It is nearly a full century since Berkeley, bishop of Cloyne, turning towards this fair land which we now inhabit, the eyes of a prophet, closed a few lines of poetical inspiration with this memorable prediction: "Time's noblest empire is the last:"[1] 1

A prediction which, to those of us whose lot has been cast by divine Providence in these regions, contains not only a precious promise, but a solemn injunction of duty, since upon our energies, and upon those of our posterity its fulfilment will depend. For, with reference to what principle could it be, that Berkeley proclaimed this, the last, to be the noblest empire 2

1 Adams is referring to George Berkeley, who served as Bishop of Cloyne in the Church of Ireland from 1734 – 1753. A famous philosopher, Berkeley founded the school of "immaterialism" which believes that the physical substances we perceive with our senses are mere ideas and cannot exist without our perception. Adams is quoting the final line of a poem by Berkeley entitled: "Verses on the Prospect of Planting Arts and Learning In America." The last four lines of the poem are as follows: "Westward the course of empire takes its way; The first four acts already past, A fifth shall close the drama with the day; Time's noblest offspring is the last." Adams uses the argument of the poem as the launching point for the entire speech that follows – even though he slightly misquotes the original text.

of time? It was, as he himself declares, on the transplantation of *learning and the arts* to America. Of learning and the arts. The four first acts – the empires of the old world, and of former ages – the Assyrian, the Persian, the Grecian, the Roman empires – were empires of conquest; dominions of man over man. The empire which his great mind, piercing into the darkness of futurity, foretold in America, was the empire of learning and the arts – the dominion of man over himself, and over physical nature – acquired by the inspirations of genius, and the toils of industry; not watered with the tears of the widow and the orphan; not cemented in the blood of human victims; founded not in discord, but in harmony – of which the only spoils are the imperfection of nature, and the victory achieved is the improvement of the condition of all. Well may this be termed nobler than the empire of conquest, in which man subdues only his fellow-men.

3 To the accomplishment of this prophecy the first necessary step was the acquisition of the right of self-government by the people of the British North American colonies, achieved by the Declaration of Independence, and its acknowledgment by the British nation. The second was the union of all these colonies under one general confederated government – a task more arduous than that of the preceding separation, but at last effected by the present constitution of the United States.

4 The third step, more arduous still than either or both the others, was that which we, fellow citizens, may now congratulate ourselves, our country, and the world of man, that it is taken. It is the adaptation of the powers, physical, moral, and intellectual, of this whole union, to the improvement of its own condition: of its moral and political condition, by wise and liberal institutions – by the cultivation of the understanding and the heart – by academies, schools, and learned institutes – by the pursuit and patronage of learning and the arts: of its physical condition, by associated labor to improve the bounties, and to supply the deficiencies of nature; to stem the torrent in its course; to level the mountain with the plain; to disarm and fetter the raging surge of the ocean. Undertakings, of which the language I now hold is no exaggerated description, have become happily familiar, not only to the conceptions, but to the enterprise, of our countrymen.[2] That, for the commencement of which we are here assembled, is eminent among

2 The preceding sentences outline the policy priorities of the Adams presidency: a national university, infrastructure investment, international exploration, and the construction of scientific institutions.

the number. The project contemplates a conquest over physical nature, such as has never yet been achieved by man. The wonders of the ancient world, the pyramids of Egypt, the Colossus of Rhodes, the temple Ephesus, the mausoleum of Artemisia, the wall of China, sink into insignificance before it – insignificance in the mass and momentum of human labor, required for the execution – insignificance in the comparison of the purposes to be accomplished by the work when executed. It is, therefore, a pleasing contemplation to those sanguine and patriotic spirits who have so long looked with hope to the completion of this undertaking, that it unites the moral power and resources – first, of numerous individuals – secondly, of the corporate cities of Washington, Georgetown, and Alexandria – thirdly, of the great and powerful states of Pennsylvania, Virginia, and Maryland – and, lastly, by the subscription authorised at the recent session of congress, of the whole union.

Friends and fellow laborers. We are informed by the *holy* oracles 5
of truth, that, at the creation of man, male and female, the lord of the universe, their Maker, blessed them, and said unto them, be fruitful and multiply, and replenish the earth, *and subdue it.*[3] To subdue the earth was, therefore, one of the first duties assigned to man at his creation; and now, in his fallen condition, it remains among the most excellent of his occupations. To subdue the earth is pre-eminently the purpose of the undertaking, to the accomplishment of which the first stroke of the spade is now to be struck. That it is to be struck by this hand, I invite you to witness – [Here the stroke of the spade][4] – and in performing this act, I call upon you to join me in fervent supplication to Him from whom that primitive injunction came, that he would follow with his blessing this joint effort of our great community, to perform his will in the subjugation of the earth

3 This is a quotation from Genesis 1:28.

4 The newspaper article in which this speech was originally released to the public includes this footnote: "Attending this action was an incident which produced a greater sensation than any other that occurred during the day. The spade which the president held struck a root, which prevented its penetrating the earth. Not deterred by trifling obstacles from doing what he had deliberately resolved to perform, Mr. Adams tried it again, with no better success. Thus foiled, he threw down the spade, hastily stripped off and laid aside his coat, and went seriously to work. The multitude around, and on the hills and trees, who could not hear, because of their distance from the open space, but could see and understand, observing this action, raised a loud and unanimous cheering, which continued for sometime after Mr. Adams had mastered the difficulty."

for the improvement of the condition of man. That he would make it one of his chosen instruments for the preservation, prosperity, and perpetuity of our union. That he would have in his holy keeping all the workmen by whose labors it is to be completed. That their lives and their health may be precious in his sight; and that they may live to see the work of their hands contribute to the comforts and enjoyments of millions of their countrymen. Friends and brethren: Permit me further to say, that I deem the duty, now performed at the request of the president and directors of the Chesapeake and Ohio Canal Company, and the corporations of the District of Columbia, one of the most fortunate incidents of my life. Though not among the functions of my official station, I esteem it as a privilege conferred upon me by my fellow-citizens of the district.[5] Called, in the performance of my service heretofore as one of the representatives of my native commonwealth; in the senate, and now as a member of the executive department of the government, my abode has been among the inhabitants of the district longer than at any other spot upon earth. In availing myself of this occasion to return to them my thanks for the numberless sets of kindness that I have experienced at their hands, may I be allowed to assign it as a motive operating upon the heart, and superadded to my official obligations, for taking a deep interest in their welfare and prosperity. Among the prospects of futurity which we may indulge the rational hope of seeing realized by this junction of distant waters, that of the auspicious influence which it will exercise over the fortunes of every portion of this district, is one upon which my mind dwells with unqualified pleasure. It is my earnest prayer that they may not be disappointed.

6 It was observed that the first step towards the accomplishment of the glorious destinies of our country was the Declaration of Independence. That the second was the union of these states under our federative government. The third is irrevocably fixed by the act upon the commencement of which we are now engaged. What time more suitable for this operation could have been selected than the anniversary of our great national festival? What place more appropriate from whence to proceed, than that which bears the name of the citizen warrior who led our armies in that

5 As president of the United States, Adams was not automatically entitled to speak at the launching of largely private economic endeavors. However, for his tireless support of the canal project – including securing additional congressional funding for the construction of the canal – the company board invited Adams to be the key guest at the groundbreaking ceremony.

eventful contest to the field, and who first presided as the chief magistrate of our union? You know that, of this very undertaking, he was one of the first protectors; and if, in the world of spirits, the affections of our mortal existence still retain their sway, may we not, without presumption, imagine that he looks down with complacency and delight upon the scene before and around us?

But, while indulging a sentiment of joyous exultation, at the benefits 7
to be derived from this labor of our friends and neighbors, let us not forget that the spirit of internal improvement is catholic and liberal. We hope and believe that its practical advantages will be extended to every individual in our union. In praying for the blessing of heaven upon our task, we ask it with equal zeal and sincerity upon every other similar work in this confederation; and particularly upon that which, on this same day, and perhaps at this very hour, is commencing from a neighboring city. It is one of the happiest characteristics in the principle of internal improvement, that the success of one great enterprise, instead of counteracting, gives assistance to the execution of another. May they increase and multiply, till, in the sublime language of inspiration, every valley shall be exalted, and every mountain and hill shall be made low; the crooked straight; the rough places plain. Thus shall the prediction of the bishop of Cloyne be converted from prophecy into history, and, in the virtues and fortunes of our posterity, the last shall prove the noblest empire of time.

Chapter 2:
Discourse on Education
(1840)

Few American presidents have possessed as strong a dedication to education as John Quincy Adams. Tutored by some of the best minds in the world, he committed much of his life to the continuous acquisition of knowledge – voraciously devouring books on science, politics, poetry, literature, religion, and every other subject under the sun. As president, Adams called for the creation of a national university to expand America's intellectual horizons and raise a new generation of well-educated public servants. Though he failed in that effort, when invited to speak at a public gathering in Braintree (now Quincy), Massachusetts, he used the opportunity to lay out a robust philosophy of education. In a complete refutation of contemporary approaches to education, Adams wastes none of his time on pedagogical methods. Instead, he takes his readers through the history of human enlightenment in Europe and North America. In the process, he shows the true purpose of education – a freer and more virtuous people.

1 The celebrated Historian of England, David Hume, in the account of his life written in the 65th year of his age by himself says, "I am, or rather *was* (for that is the style I must now use in speaking of myself, which emboldens me the more I speak my sentiments); I *was*, I say, a man of mild disposition," &c. then giving his own character, according to his own estimate of it.[1]

2 Men and women of Braintree! I have lived eight years longer in this world of vicissitudes and cares, than David Hume had lived when he felt himself bound to assume this style, and when he considered it as investing him with the privilege of speaking more boldly his sentiments, than he might have done while speaking in the present tense.

1 This is a quotation from David Hume's autobiographical essay, "My Own Life." Hume wrote this essay when he was sixty-five – a fact which Adams uses as an opening to mention his own age of seventy-three.

Am I not then authorized by his example, to invert the order of his transition from the present to the past, and to say – I *was* or rather I *am* one of yourselves? I *was* born at Braintree; and in the revolution of time, I *am*, one of the oldest inhabitants of that Town. In Braintree I first beheld the light of Heaven – first breathed the atmosphere of your granite rocks – first sucked with my mother's milk the love of Liberty, and the reverence for the Gospel of truth. In early childhood, in the midst of the storm of the war of Independence, in the dead of Winter, I embarked at the very spot where your forefathers landed at the foot of Mount Wollaston – I embarked, with a father, upon the tempestuous ocean, for realms beyond the Atlantic tide; defying the battle and the breeze for the cause of your Country. Since then, for a space of forty years I led a wandering life, in distant regions; always in the service of your fathers or in yours; always grateful to Heaven for having made me a Braintree boy, and always feeling the sentiments, which once on losing sight of the blue hills in your neighborhood, I committed to paper in the following lines: 3

And you, ye distant hills of blue –
To whom I bid, with bosom burning,
When wending far, my last Adieu;
And first to greet mine eyes returning ;
Oh! how shall speech in words convey,
Words, the heart holds not in derision,
The *pang* that points your parting ray,
The *bliss* that wings your meeting vision.[2]

Let me then in addressing you, fellow citizens of Braintree, say I *was* or rather I *am* a native of the town of Braintree, and let that be your motive for indulging me with the freedom of speech – with more boldness than I might presume to use, if I came among you as a stranger. 4

And I make this appeal to your kind and indulgent feelings because I shall need it. David Hume took it as a warrant of authority to speak his sentiments boldly, because at the age of 65 he claimed to be a man of a former age: restrained by none of those prudential considerations which 5

2 This seems to be a poem of Adams' own invention. A prolific poet, Adams' published works in this genre achieved great notoriety during his own lifetime but have since fallen into obscurity.

admonish a speaker in addressing the public to abstain from exciting topics, and to say nothing with which the prepossessions of his hearers might not cordially sympathize – Yet he had not then attained, and never reached the allotted boundary of old age to man – the three score years and ten of his earthly pilgrimage; which I have already passed. I have then a stronger claim than his upon the mere score of age to speak my sentiments boldly, and that which is thus my right becomes my imperious and overruling duty, towards you the inhabitants of my native town, of which through all the wanderings of a long and eventful life, I have never ceased in the sincerity of my soul to say:

"Where'er I roam, whatever realms I see,
My heart untravell'd fondly turns to thee."[3]

6 When I undertook the arduous, but not unwelcome task of addressing you in public, it was intimated to me that it might be agreeable to you to hear me upon that most interesting subject to you and to your posterity, the education of your children; and the desire of discoursing to you upon the theme, not less than in the manner the most acceptable to yourselves, was of strong prevailment to induce a ready compliance with that intimation.

7 But what could I possibly say to you for the advancement of the cause of education which you do not habitually say to yourselves? –We are almost daily celebrating in every part of New England, the accomplishment of two centuries since the first gathering of a church or the incorporation of a town. A few weeks only have past away since the filial reverence of the descendants from the first founders of the church and religious society at Mount Wollaston, paid this tribute of commemoration to the virtues of their forefathers – and within the compass of another year it is your purpose to strew flowers over the sepulchres of those patriarchs of our land by a similar festival to keep in remembrance the founder of our primitive town of Braintree. We have embalmed anew the venerable remains of our first Pastor and Teacher William Thomson and Henry Flint; but there is an incident connected with the history of the latter, not less precious than any other memorial in his individual life. On his grave stone, yet standing in the cemetery of the church in Quincy, of which he was a principal founder, is yet legible the following record – "Here lies interred the body of

3 A quotation from Oliver Goldsmith's poem "The Traveller; or, a Prospect of Society."

the Rev. Mr. Henry Flint, who came to New England in the year 1635, was ordained the first teacher of the church of Braintray 1639, and died April 27, 1668. He had the character of a gentlemen, remarkable for his piety, learning, wisdom and fidelity in his office." Men and women of Braintree! had the monumental inscription upon the tomb of the beloved *instructor* and spiritual monitor, counselor and guide, of your forefather pilgrims of the first cisatlantic generation terminated here, might I not have invited you to pause and meditate – to inquire how much of the peace, how much of the earthly happiness, how much of the piety and virtue, how much of the eternal welfare of your ancestors of five generations, of yourselves, of your children and your children's children to the end of time, may be directly and indirectly traced to those qualities thus testified as characteristics of this venerable man? – But the blessed memorial stops not here, it proceeds – "By him on his right hand lies the body of Margery, his beloved consort who died March 1686-7. Her maiden name was Hoar. She was a gentlewoman of piety, prudence, and peculiarly accomplished for instructing young gentlewomen, many being sent to her from other towns, especially from Boston." Women of Braintree, let me now appeal to you! If I was authorized to inquire how highly is to be estimated by your townsmen of the present generation, the blessing of being descended from fathers who were fed with the nourishment of the bread of life by a shepherd of souls so distinguished as the first teacher of Braintree Church, how much more emphatically may I ask the same question of you, who in addition to the enjoyment of the same benefits, may look back to the matrons of the town from its first foundation, as blest with the means of education suited to the tenderness, the refinement and delicacy of their sex. The solicitude of the first fathers of New England for the education of their sons has been among their brightest claims to renown in all succeeding ages. And shall it not be among the garlands of glory to the women of Braintree, that in the roll of their primitive mothers, the wife of their first pastor was not only eminent as an instructress of wisdom and virtue, but that her services to the age and land in which she lived, were so worthily appreciated by her surviving contemporary inhabitants of the town, that their grateful acknowledgment and remembrance of them yet lives and breathes and speaks to us all, from the assembled multitude of the surrounding dead, and from the voice of her husband's tomb.

8 It is an opinion universally entertained that the first and great impulse to the settlement of New England was *Religion*. But has it been sufficiently considered, and may I be permitted to inquire, whether Religion is not herself the child of *Education*, and whether it would not be more proper to say, that *Education* was from its first origin the governing principle of the settlement of New England, or in other words that Education was the mother of New England?

9 What is *Religion?* It is not the sentiment in the heart of man, of his own immortal nature, and of his responsibility to a tribunal not of earth for his conduct upon earth. The existence of a God; the immortality of the human soul, and future retribution, are the elements of what is called Natural Religion – but even these first principles are not of spontaneous growth in the human heart. They are the fruits of *Education* – they must be taught. They were revealed by God himself to the first created man, and to his partner in the Garden of Eden, and they are still taught to Christians of all denominations in the Mosaic narrative of the Creation.

10 But this is not the Religion which prompted the settlement of New England – for this is a creed common to the Christian, Mohammedan and Jew throughout the habitable globe. The first settlers of New England were Christians of the most straitest sect. Their text-book was the Bible; a book written by various authors – in different periods of the world – the latest, sixteen hundred years remote, at the time of the settlement of New England, and all, in languages no longer extant save in the memory of the profoundly learned.

11 In this book were contained the history of the human race from the creation of the world; a rule of faith, for the relations between man and his Maker; a rule of life, for the government of his relations with his fellow creature man – and the glorious gospel of the blessed God. But in the wise and inscrutable dispensations of Providence, this book of divine inspiration for its composition had been committed to the uninspired intellect of man for its construction. What the meaning was of any one statement of fact, principle, sentiment or opinion contained in it, was to be ascertained by the ordinary operation of the human mind. It was mind impressed upon paper in the character of the alphabet. But the first five books of this compilation, the Pentateuch, or five books of Moses, had been written very recently after the first invention of alphabetical writing, and contained in that mode of incorporating thought two thousand years of history before the existence of

that invention; when the narrative of events, and the lessons of morals, and the precepts of instruction must necessarily have been delivered from mind to mind, by some other mode of conveyance. It is well known that before the invention of alphabetical writing, the Egyptian records were kept in what was called hieroglyphics, or an art of expressing thought by imagery. Writing was the picture of thought. Material substances were thus represented by their portraiture, a man, a horse, a bird, a fish. The sun, moon and stars, mountains, trees and rivers, every object in nature visible to the eye, could be represented to the eye, by imitation.

In the progress of human improvement certain properties were observed 12
invariably to belong to certain material substances, and by common agreement the material substance was exhibited for the property belonging to it. Hence the extension of the art of hieroglyphic writing, and I submit to your consideration a conjecture which has often occurred to me, that the account of the creation in the book of Genesis, was only a transfer to alphabetic writing, of more ancient Egyptian memorials in hieroglyphics. For we are expressly told that Moses was learned in all the wisdom of the Egyptians, and this may account for the representation of the Spirit of evil in the form of a Serpent, and for that of life, and for the knowledge of good and evil, abstractions of the mind, in the shape of trees growing in the garden of Paradise.

Be this however as it may, the books of Moses are written in the Hebrew 13
language, a dialect of the Phœnician; as it was spoken by the children of Israel at the time of their emigration from Egypt about fifteen hundred years before the birth of Christ. The subsequent historical books, from Joshua, the immediate successor of Moses, to Ezra and Nehemiah, contain the history of more than one thousand years, in the same language, modified from age to age, through the long lapse of years, and by the intermixture of the children of Israel with the various nations of Palestine, and with the Assyrians, Babylonians, Medes and Persians, by whom they were successively subdued and carried into captivity. The Psalms of David, as they are called, but really of him and of several other writers ranging through a period of a thousand years, the Proverbs, the Canticles, and the Ecclesiastes of Solomon, and the solemn and awful revelations from Heaven committed to writing by seventeen prophets, are in the same language, with an intermixture of the Chaldaic in the books composed after the Babylonian captivity. All the Books of the New Testament, as originally composed, are

in the Greek language, and there are translations of all the Books of the Old Testament into the Greek and Latin languages, of so great antiquity, that by the vast majority of the Christian world they are considered in all respects of equal, and in some passages of superior authority to the Hebrew.

14 These books, thus composed, are universally admitted, by all Christians of all denominations, as containing a rule of faith and a rule of life for all human kind. But, considered merely as history, they relate a series of events almost entirely miraculous, that is of special interpositions of divine Providence, suspending the ordinary laws of physical nature, and operating by preternatural agency. Considered as prophecies, their predictions are darkly and mysteriously blended with their history – and there is among Christians great diversity of opinion, with regard to the import and meaning of the prophecies – diversities which have given rise to bitter controversies, to furious dissensions, and to cruel, bloody and exterminating wars.

15 The Founder of the Christian religion himself, promised a Redeemer of mankind from the transgression of their first parents in paradise – promised by a covenant of Almighty God with Abraham the father of the faithful, in the clear, explicit and repeated declaration that in his seed all the families of the earth should be blessed – promised again to his son Isaac, and to his son Jacob – promised through a long succession of ages, to Moses, to Daniel, to Solomon, to a long line of prophets and of kings – the Founder of the Christian religion himself, was crucified as a malefactor – numbered with the transgressors of that very law which he came to fulfill and to abolish. He suffered the ignominious death of the Cross, but the sentence of the law, delivered from Sinai, as understood and expounded by the high priest instituted by that divine dispensation.

16 But this crucified Galilean, was the Saviour of the world – the Redeemer promised at the expulsion of Adam from Paradise. In a career of four years of manhood immediately preceding his death, he had unfolded to the world of mankind a new *rule of life* – a complete system of morals, founded upon two first principles; two elementary ideas. The one, was life and immortality, or in other words, the resurrection. The other, was the law of brotherly love, founded upon the principle of the natural equality of mankind and the resulting principle of peace on earth, good will to men, and the duty of universal application of doing unto others as you would that they should do unto you. In these two elementary principles, all Christians of all denominations concur. Whoever derides or disbelieves them or either of

them can have no claims to the title of a Christian. It was not indeed for the promulgation of either of these doctrines that he suffered death. It was for the assertion of his own authority as the promised Messiah, for the declaration that he was the Son of God – that he possessed and exercised the power of performing miracles, and of forgiving sins; and for the unqualified assertion, that if they should put him to death he would by his own resurrection and ascension within three days, prove the truth of his doctrine of immortal life. He was accordingly sentenced to death, and the sentence was executed in strict conformity to the Law of Moses as it was understood by the Priests, the Scribes and Pharisees, the Minister and Interpreters of the Law. And as he foretold, on the third day from his crucifixion he rose again from the dead, was seen and conversed with by hundreds of his disciples for the space of forty days; and then leaving them with the explicit declaration that all power was given unto him in heaven and in earth, and with the express command *therefore*, to go and *teach* all nations, baptizing them in the name of the Father, and of the Son, and of the Holy Ghost – *teaching* them, to observe all things whatsoever he had commanded the disciples, and with the promise that he would be with them always, even unto the end of the world.

Christian brethren and sisters! when I undertook to discourse to you 17
upon the subject of *Education* – upon the first superficial survey of my subject, under a sort of prepossession, that considerations connected with your temporal and worldly welfare would be the only motives proper to be presented by a layman to your minds, I naturally inquired of myself, as at the entrance of this address I have inquired of you, what I could possibly say to you for the promotion of the cause of education, which you do not daily and habitually say to yourselves? But when, desirous of presenting in front the argument which could operate at once upon your hearts and minds, I turned my thoughts to the principles and impulses which had influenced and directed your venerable ancestors, the first settlers of New England, the first and overruling motive, which stood forth in prominent relief as the corner-stone of their History was *Religion* – the Christian *Religion* – And as this was not simply the Religion of Nature, but peculiarly the Religion of a *Book*, the first reference to that Book, its history and character, immediately disclosed the source of that deep and intense interest, that fervid and unceasing anxiety, which glowed in the bosoms of all the first founders of New England. The Religion of the Bible must be *taught*.

It must be instilled into the mind of childhood, and believed even before it is understood. Worldly motive and interests, have been the exclusive or the predominating influences to the settlement of all other colonial establishments known to the history of mankind. The only exception of ancient history was the emigration of Abraham from Ur of Chaldea, and the subsequent exodus of his descendants, the children of Israel, from Egypt to settle in the promised land. They carried with them a Code of Laws delivered by God himself to Moses upon Mount Sinai, which they accepted by an express and formal covenant, often repeated by their posterity, and binding upon them through all the vicissitudes of their fortunes, till the promised Mediator of the New Covenant appeared in the person of Jesus of Nazareth. He came among them, declaring himself as having existed before Abraham, as commissioned expressly by his Father and their Father, by his God and their God, to deliver to them a *New Law*, to fulfill and partially supersede the Law delivered from Sinai. He came claiming to be their prophet, priest and king – but he declared that his kingdom was not of this world – It was the kingdom of Heaven – It was the resurrection from death to immortal life, - and his new Law – his new command – first to his own people, the children of Israel, and then to the whole race of man in that and all succeeding ages – was the Law of Love, That they should *love one another*.

18 This simple and all-pervading principle was not in the Law of Moses. It was not in any preexisting code of Laws ever imposed upon men. It was buried in the heart of man, blended and surrounded with every selfish and sordid passion to which his fall from Paradise had surrendered him. But it was *there*, and Jesus who knew what was in man brought it forth, and proclaimed it as the transcendent and paramount Law of man's nature. At the same time he told his disciples, that as a test of his principles he must himself suffer a cruel and ignominious death – a death reserved for malefactors and slaves. He told them, that they must all expect for proclaiming the glad tidings of his gospel to share his fate and suffer like him – That their own hearts were so incrusted with evil passions, and perverse customs and traditions, that they themselves did not fully comprehend the extent and universality of his Law – That to conform their practice to it, they must be regenerated, must be born again, and become entirely new men – That they themselves knew not what spirit they were of, and that devoted to him and his doctrines as they declared and believed themselves to be, they would all desert and deny him at his last hour – as they did.

But he gave in his own person the proof of his doctrine of resurrection from the dead – and after that event, he promised them the Holy Ghost, as a Comforter for all they had suffered, and all they had yet to endure, and commanded them to go forth and *teach* all nations *to observe* whatsoever things he had commanded them. 19

Now this *teaching* of the commandments of Christ, to be observed by all nations, was by the express terms of the commission, recorded in the Gospel of St. Matthew, to continue to the end of the world – and wherever the Christian religion is established, this *teaching* must be to *children*, and it must continue through life. For it is not only doctrine but observance that must be taught – Faith and Works. 20

The doctrine of immortal life, is so congenial to the heart even of unregenerate man; it is so soothing even to his selfish passions, that it is easily believed by all to whom it is *taught*. Though not explicitly revealed in the Old Testament, it was believed, not as an article of faith, but as a speculative opinion by the generality of the Jewish nation; excepting by the sect of the Sadducees,[4] who denied it altogether. A clear, undoubting conviction of it, is the first article of the Christian faith, and it is accordingly taught by Christians of every denomination. A future state of retribution, a resurrection of bliss to all who have done good, and of condemnation to all who have done evil, is also a fundamental article of Christianity, although the particular nature of the happiness to be enjoyed, and the nature and extent of the condemnation to be endured, have not been explicitly revealed. 21

But the doctrine of eternal life, is not the only lesson to be taught by the disciples of Jesus to all nations, to the end of the world – it is to be taught in connection indissoluble with the new commandment, to love one another. Among his last words at the table of the Passover immediately before his death, he gave this *new* commandment – and repeating it expressly said, "by *this* shall all men know that ye are my disciples, if ye have love one to another." 22

This precept, too, was understood by all his apostles, as embracing the whole substance of his commands – nor has it ever been questioned by any human being, recognizing his authority as a divine teacher of religion and morals. 23

And with these two principles universally received by all who call upon the name of Christ, and acknowledge him as their Lord and Master, how 24

---

4 Adams is referencing a historical set of Jewish faithful who denied the existence of an afterlife and in the New Testament challenge Jesus of Nazareth on this point.

is it comprehensible, that this religion of awful responsibility to God for the observance of universal benevolence to man, should have been for more than sixteen hundred years, from the day of Christ's passion till the settlement of New England, the source and cause from age to age of the bloodiest and most desolating wars that ever afflicted the human race. By what unaccountable perversity in the composition of the animal man, the only animated being on the face of the terraqueous globe, endowed by his Creator with the faculty of reason, is it, that the religion of Conscience and of Love, of glory to God in the highest, and of peace on earth, good will to men, should in the process of its operations on the heart and mind of man towards that consummation of its destiny, promised and intended by its Founder, when the practice of Christians shall correspond with the Christian faith, and all the kingdoms of the earth shall become the kingdoms of the Lord Jesus Christ, have been doomed to make its way through oceans of blood – through ages of persecution, through hatred and revenge, through bigotry and superstition, through avarice and ambition, through fraud and hypocrisy, through lust and pride, through fanaticism and delusion, through all that the Spirit of evil can devise and all that fallen man, the compound of the tiger and the fox can perpetrate, to that serene empyrean of Heaven upon earth, when the Lion shall lie down with the Lamb, when the swords shall be beaten into ploughshares and the spears into pruning hooks – when nation shall no longer rise against nation, neither shall they learn war any more ?

25 Christian Friends! – The radical cause of this deplorable inconsistency, and of all this melancholy depravity in the History of Mankind is defective *Education.* That the human heart is deceitful above all things, and desperately wicked, had been said by divine inspiration, hundreds of years before the birth of the Redeemer, nor until his appearance upon earth had there been any improvement in its condition. Jesus was a *teacher* sent from God, to *reveal* the doctrine of immortal life and future retribution, and to *teach* the way on earth to eternal blessedness in Heaven.

26 But when the *teacher* has done his part, there remains to be performed the part of the *learner*. It was never promised by Jesus or his Apostles that the system of faith and of morals which he *taught*, should be forthwith received, understood and practiced upon by all mankind. In confirmation of his doctrine of immortality, and to authenticate his mission from heaven, he performed miracles, or as he called them, mighty works. In

illustration of the practice which he commanded his disciples to observe and to teach, he spoke in parable for the space of four years, disclosing even in minute detail the practical application of his *new* commandment of mutual love, to all the ordinary concerns of human life. But he came to *teach*, and not to compel. His Law was a Law of Liberty. He left the human mind and human action free, and the first lesson that he gave to his disciples was that he came to revolutionize the very nature of man – to regenerate him from the womb – to extirpate from his bosom all the evil passions to which he had been surrendered by the disobedience of his first parents to the commandment of God, and to *purify* unto himself a peculiar people, zealous of good works. But he gave them no encouragement to hope that this revolution in the very nature of man would be immediately or even speedily accomplished. He forewarned them that he must himself suffer death in confirmation of his mission by the treachery of one of themselves. He announced and bewailed the impending ruin and destruction of Chorazin, of Bethsaida, of Jerusalem herself, for the hardness of the hearts of their people, who despised his authority, and rejected his commands. He told them plainly that they should have persecution in the world in proportion to their fidelity to him, and that he came not to bring Peace upon earth but a sword.

A sword say you? for what? for what but for self-defense? He brought 27
it not for conquest – for tyranny or oppression – but he brought it to be used by his disciples for their own defence, in their conflicts with the world against the tyranny and oppression of others. He was himself put to death, as he had foretold he should be, and upon his trial, rebuked one of his earliest disciples, for using the sword that he had bought, not in self-defence, but in useless and furious animosity against a servant of the high priest.

In the execution of the command which he gave them after his resur- 28
rection and immediately before his ascension, to go forth and *teach* all nations till the end of the world to observe all the commands which he had delivered to them – they went forth and *taught*. For the space of more than three hundred years, they met in return for this teaching, persecution, martyrdom, and cruel death. Still they taught – and still according to that beautiful parable of their Lord and Master, of the sower and the seed – although much of their seed fell by the way side and was devoured by the fowls of the air, much upon stony places, where it could take no root, but sprang up and under a scorching sun, soon withered away; much

among thorns, which sprang up and chocked them – yet other fell upon good ground, and brought forth fruit, some a hundred fold, some sixty fold, some thirty fold. And thus, under ten successive merciless decrees of so many Roman Emperors, masters of the world, prohibiting upon pain of death, this *teaching* of the disciples of Jesus, it was still making its way into the heart of man, irresistibly superseding the institutions of the Levitical Law, undermining and overthrowing the idolatrous worship of the Roman Empire, and prostrating before the simple command of mutual love from the lips of the Teacher of Nazareth, all the thrones and dominion, principalities and powers of the Earth.

29 At length after more than three hundred years of proscription and persecution, the religion of Jesus ascended the imperial throne of the Cæsars, and was proclaimed mistress of the world. But alas! the seed which until then had fallen by the way side and been devoured by the fowl of the air, was now destined to fall upon stony places, to spring up without root, and to wither away under the scorching sun of imperial power. Constantine adopted and professed and ordained the Christian religion, not in its own spirit of obedience to God and love to man, but as an instrument of conquest – as a weapon of war. He had seen or pretended to have seen a vision of a crucifix, at noon-day, transcending the light of the sun, and bearing the legible inscription in the Greek language – "By this, conquer." It was in the midst of a formidable war that this supernatural apparition presented itself to his eyes, which a cotemporary Christian historian, Eusebius, bishop of Cæsarea, declares was related by Constantine to himself many years after, confirmed by the solemnity of an oath. But whether this vision was the result of a fanatical delusion imposing upon the optical nerves of Constantine himself, or whether it was a fraudulent and deliberate imposture, it carried with it internal evidence, that the establishment of Christianity upon the throne of the world, was not in the true spirit of the Redeemer, life, immortality and brotherly love, but war, hatred and *conquest.* Constantine therefore stripped from all the warlike standards of the empire the bird of prey, the Roman Eagle; and supplied his place with the Labarum, the conquering and unconquerable emblem of the cross – and thenceforth the banners of the cross themselves became the banners of fraud and imposture, and the standard of a crucified Saviour, was waved over embattled legions marching to conquest, instead of peaceful disciples *teaching* all nations the law of immortal life and of brotherly love.

And upon this vicious foundation was soon erected a system of eccle- 30
siastical hierarchy, in the progress of which the bishops of Rome, assuming to be the successors of Saint Peter, with the pastoral staff of a shepherd and the ring of a fisherman, arrogated to themselves a dominion over their brethren of the Christian faith, to which no sovereign of earthly origin ever presumed to aspire. From *teachers* of the gospel of Christ they were gradually metamorphosed by the ascendancy which they acquired over the minds of men, not only into sovereign temporal princes, but into the superior beings, exempt from all the infirmities of human nature, invested with absolute and uncontrollable power, armed with the authority of setting up and putting down kings, of absolving subjects from the ties of allegiance to their sovereigns, of laying whole nations under interdict, and of distributing at their discretion all the territories of the earth; and to cap the climax of blasphemy, not only to forgive and redeem from punishment the transgressions of men, but to grant for money indulgences for the perpetration of crimes. Can it be conceived as possible that this abominable system of fraud and imposture was actually consummated, originating in the adoption of Christianity by Constantine, commencing by small and imperceptible beginnings, but swelling and expanding into portentous immensity, for the space of nearly twelve hundred years, till the appointed day of Martin Luther.

And during the same period, some of the seeds fell among thorns, 31
which grew up with them and choked them – thorns of internal dissension and thorns of external war. Rival ambition had manifested itself among the twelve apostles of Jesus, even while he lived ; nor was it wholly extinguished by his severe admonition that they knew not what spirit they were of. Immediately after his decease, irritating debates and sharp animosities sprung up among them – multitudes of the Jewish converts maintaining that the whole Levitical law continued unrepealed, and the proselytes from the gentiles inflexibly refusing to submit to the rite of circumcision, or to restrict themselves to the distinction between clean and unclean meats, or to encumber themselves with the burthensome ritual of the Mosaic law. In the Instructions of Jesus to his disciples, he had dwelt with emphatic solemnity upon the indispensable necessity of *Faith* in him and his doctrines, for admission to the kingdom of Heaven and for salvation to their immortal souls – but the law which he gave was a law of universal love, and no stronger evidence of Faith in him could be exhibited than by implicit observance

of that Law. Now *Faith*, in the sense in which it was required by Jesus of his disciples, has been defines by the Apostle of the Gentiles "the substance of things hoped for, and the evidence of things not seen." It is *belief* – a property of man's immortal soul, possessed by no other being upon earth. For belief gives to future time the anticipated certainty of the past – it annihilates time and space, and is the most power of all the arguments of natural religion to prove the immortal nature of man. Well then might Jesus and his Apostles, in their teaching of mankind, dwell upon the transcendent importance and irresistible efficacy of this *passive faith*, this firm belief in the divine mission of the Saviour and in the promises of his gospel, for there is another property of *faith*, by which it regulates the conduct of men. This is active faith, and is the foundation of all the moral relations between man and his fellow creature man. This faith in action, is the adamantine chain which holds the moral elements of the world together. Faith in its passive sense may be considered as synonymous with confidence – in its active sense with *fidelity*. The definition of faith by St. Paul in the 11th chapter of the Epistle to the Hebrews, is of passive faith – and he says elsewhere that it comes by hearing – and hearing by the word of God.[5] But all the illustrations throughout the whole of that chapter of the unbounded power of faith, consist of its efficacy to the production of works; as confidence in God; as passive faith – *belief* in the omnipotence and goodness of God.

32 You have all observed, my friends, in reading and comparing together the strong language of St. Paul in urging this all comprehensive power and influence of faith, with that of his brother Apostle James in the second chapter of his Epistle, where he seems to represent *faith* as altogether subordinate to works; there is an apparent difference between the two Apostles, as to the sense in which they understand the term Faith.[6] The difference is only apparent. The definition of St. Paul is strictly confined to faith in its passive sense, as synonymous with *belief* – confidence in God – but all

5 The exact definition given by St. Paul at the very start of Hebrews 11 is: "Now faith is the assurance of things hoped for, the conviction of things not seen. For by it the people of old received their condemnation. By faith we understand that the universe was created by the word of God, so that what is seen was not made out of things that are visible."

6 The apostle James on the other hand defines faith thus: "But what good is it, my brothers, if someone says he has faith but does not have works? Can that faith save him? If a brother or sister is poorly clothed and lacking in daily food, and one of you says to them, "Go in peace, be warmed and filled," without giving them the things they need for the body, what good is that? So also faith by itself, if it does not have works, is dead."

his illustrations, both special from Abel to Samuel and the prophets, and general, of the sufferings endured and of wonders performed by the faithful, are all, without a single exception, instances of faith manifested by works. So that St. James, who so emphatically declares that faith without works is dead, and that the devils *believe* and tremble, manifestly refers only to that faith which is synonymous with *belief*, while St. Paul as manifestly refers to that faith which is synonymous with fidelity – the faith which is manifested in action, by the performance of good works. There is therefore no real difference between the doctrines of the two Apostles; but need I tell you that there was a difference, a deep and radical difference of impression upon the minds of the disciples who heard them, with regard to this doctrine of faith and works, which after a lapse of nearly nineteen hundred years yet remains unadjusted, and which even now may expose me to the suspicion of heresy for this simple statement of my own view of the case. I pray you to understand that I am not about to involve myself or you in the controversy between Faith and Works – that I only speak historically; only point out to you some of the thorns of internal dissension among which the seed of the blessed gospel fell immediately after it had been sown, and in the first century of the Christian era. And then came the trials of the Apostles; the repeated imprisonments of Peter; the martyrdom of Stephen by a frantic multitude, and of James by the tyrant Herod; the cruel persecutions first inflicted and afterwards endured by Paul; the charges against the Christians of setting fire to Rome by Nero, and the long train of ten Persecutions from that time till the conversion of Constantine – while at the same time from the teeming fancies of the converts to Christianity multitudes of wild, extravagant and absurd sectarian creeds sprung up in the rank soul of the human heart, to obscure the divine light of the gospel and to choke the seed of the sower. The time will allow me barely to glance at the melancholy fertility of the successive growths of thorns which chocked the seeds of the truth as it is in Jesus, for many centuries by the imposture of Mahomet[7] founded upon the principle of inextinguishable War, in direct opposition to that of perpetual and universal Peace, the pure and simple doctrine of Christianity – or by that perversion of Christian principle generated by the false religion of the Koran, the Crusades for the recovery of the Sepulchre of Christ from the infidels, and the short lived establishment of a Christian kingdom in what was termed the holy land.

7 A now outdated spelling of Muhammad.

33 Of all these obstructions to the establishment of the peaceful kingdom of Christ upon earth, the most terrible and the most fatal, was the dominion which the bishops of Rome, in the name and as the pretended successors of Saint Peter, had usurped over the minds of men. Instead of *teaching* all nations the observance of the commands of Christ, the bishops of Rome had in a long succession of ages erected a Sovereignty for *ruling* all nations, and teaching them only the commands of men – and they ruled with a rod of iron. We all know that the reformation of this anti-Christian system was commenced by Martin Luther, and that although for ages before, ineffectual struggles against it had been crushed by its power, it was the monstrous pretension and practice of selling indulgences for the commission of crimes, which was first contested and then assailed by him as a *teacher* of nations to the observance of the commands of Christ, according to the commission given by the Saviour to his disciples at the moment preceding his ascension.

34 Of the progress of the Protestant Reformation it is impossible for me here to speak; but in discoursing to you upon the importance and the transcendent duties of education, I pray you to remark that the direct issue between the Protestant reformers and the papal usurpations was *education*. It was the freedom of thought against organized power. It had been established as one of the fundamental articles of the Catholic faith, that the Roman Pontiff – the head of the Church – was infallible – that his will was law. That the keys of Heaven had been transmitted to him in uninterrupted succession from Saint Peter, and that all other powers upon earth, were bound to implicit obedience to his decrees, issued with a fraudulent semblance of humility in the professed capacity of a servant of servants. To secure this implicit obedience to his will, the word of God itself, the Scriptures of the Old and New Testament, were withheld from the inspection of the People, and reserved to the exclusive possession of the Priesthood – for many ages not only
35 the great mass of the People, but the Rulers of the earth, kings and emperors, were not even taught to read, and when in the revolutions of time, the languages in which the Oracles of God had been composed became extinct, no translation of them into any of the languages of modern Europe had been published, until Luther with his own hand, in defiance of the papal law, made the first translation of them into German.

36 Thus one of the first consequences of the Protestant Reformation was to unlock the Holy Scriptures to the understandings of the people but that they might be qualified to receive them, it became indispensably

necessary to *teach* the great mass of the people the art of *reading*. It was also necessary that this art should be taught in childhood; not only because childhood is the period of human life best adapted to the reception of all religious impressions, but because the tenderness of affection for children had been signally manifested throughout his life by the Founder of Christianity, and because one of his most peremptory and affecting commands to his disciples had been, "Suffer little children to come unto me, and forbid them not."

Education, then, the education of children, and the art of reading, was 37
the primary impulse to the Protestant Reformation. The right of reading the Bible, was the first privilege secured to every follower of Christ, by the successful assault of Martin Luther upon the supremacy of the Church of Rome.

But the Reformation was the work of ages – it is not yet consum- 38
mated. The Bible is the word of God, the seed of righteousness upon earth, and of blessedness in the world to come. But of this seed, much still falls by the way side, much on stony places, much among thorns; and even of that which falls upon good ground, the returns are unequal, according to the richness of the soil and the variety of the seasons. Luther translated the Scriptures into the German language, and made them thus accessible to all his countrymen who could read. He was followed by a host of pious and learned men, of the other European nations, who translated the holy writings into the several languages of their respective countries, and thus the study of the Scriptures became the universal occupation of all the Christian nations. The invention of printing, which had preceded only by a few years the daring innovations of Luther, multiplied as the sands of the sea, the readers of the canonized books, and the splendid Polyglott Bible, compiled with immense labor, and published with princely magnificence by Cardinal Ximenes, furnished the learned patriarchs of the Reformation the means of correcting and improving their versions of the Old and New Testaments in the modern languages, by collating and comparing with each other not only the text of the Scriptures themselves, but the commentaries upon them and expositions of their contents, as well by the Doctors of the Jewish Sanhedrim, as by the Fathers of the Christian Church.[8]

8 Cardinal Francisco Jimenez de Cisneros was a Spanish cardinal and grand inquisitor who, among other accomplishments, organized the production of the Complutensian Polyglot Bible – the first Bible to have side by side translations of the text.

39 The seals of divine revelation were thus broken, and the Bible was opened to the inspection and examination of the Protestant Christian throughout the world. But two steps further became indispensably necessary to the full enjoyment of the inestimable treasure thus dispensed to all classes of the community. The first was *education* – by dispensing to the whole people, the knowledge of the art of reading and the second was the right of private judgement, or in other words the privilege of every reader, to exercise the faculties of his own understanding in the interpretation of what he reads.

40 And here we find the source of that inseparable connection between knowledge, and virtue and liberty, which characterized your forefathers, the Puritan settlers of New England, beyond every other people upon earth. Other Colonies have been settled under the impulse of worldly interests – of commercial enterprise – of romantic adventure for the search of gold or silver mines, or from the baser motive of ambition varnished over with zeal – the conquest of unoffending nations under the hypocritical pretense of converting them to the Christian faith.

41 The transcendent and overruling principle of the first settlers of New England, was Conscience. All the monarchies of Christendom resisted the reformation of Luther. A war of thirty years was the immediate consequence of his secession from the Church of Rome, in his native land – a war, the ravages and desolation of which still arrest the traveler over those regions in his path, with the melancholy reflection that the ruin inflicted by the hand of man, as it surpasses the destructive power, bids defiance even to the repairing hand of time. The wars of the Reformation extended over all Europe. They were modified by the political agitations and convulsions of the age. The spirit of reform was arrested in its progress by the apostacy of Henry the 4th in France – it severed from the crown of Spain the Provinces of the United Netherlands, and converted them into a Republic. It overthrew the dynasty of the Stuarts in Great Britain; brought one of its monarchs to the block; and expelled another and his family forever from the throne. In the process of these convulsions a portion of the people of England, withdrew from the field of persecution and of blood; not from any motives of worldly welfare, but to the total sacrifice of them all, for the uninterrupted enjoyment of the rights of conscience; for the privilege of holding the Holy Scriptures as their only rule of faith, and of interpreting them by the dictates of their own understanding.

Now to a colony thus composed, the education of their children was a necessary of life more indispensable than food, or raiment, or shelter. Their bodies might perish by famine, or by nakedness, or by exposure to the inclemency of winter snows and barren rocks, in a region where it has recently been said that granite and ice are the only productions of nature – but animal life, the preservation of their bodies, was to them but a secondary concern. The food for which they hungered and thirsted was for the nourishment of the spirit, and the preservation of the never dying soul. This was the Faith that came by *hearing*. The first of all their wants was *teacher* – teachers for themselves – teachers for their children. 42

Was I not then justified in saying that *Education* was the mother of New England? – that the predominating and controlling impulse which brought our forefathers from a land where they were in the enjoyment of every temporal blessing, and which they tenderly loved, as their country, to a howling wilderness where they could enjoy nothing but Conscience and Freedom, was *Education?* Such is the testimony of their History – what is the language of their Laws? 43

With the first settlers of the Massachusetts Colony, there came over learned and pious men, educated at the English Universities, and some of them among the most eminent divines of the age. On board the Arabella, the vessel in which Governor Winthrop came, religious worship was regularly performed, every Lord's day, even in the most tempestuous weather; and immediately after their departure from the coast of England, they appointed two days in the week, upon which Mr. Phillips, their minister, catechized the people. 44

On their arrival in this land, their first care was to keep a day of thanksgiving in all their plantations, and no sooner had they fixed upon the three hills as the spot for their settlement, than they formed themselves into a church, and chose Mr. Wilson their *Teacher*, Mr. Newell and Elder, and Mr. Gager and Mr. Aspenwall, Deacons. Nor is it to be forgotten that in our own town of Braintree, the gathering of the church preceded the incorporation of the town – that the primary cause of the formation of the church, was the inconvenience and sometimes impossibility for the inhabitants of Mount Wollaston to attend public worship at Boston, and that small as their number were, they chose two persons for the administration of their spiritual concerns, one under the denomination of Pastor, and the other of Teacher. 45

46 Within six years after their landing in the wilderness, four hundred pounds were given by the General Court of the Massachusetts Colony towards the establishment of a public school at Newtown, afterwards called Cambridge; and two years later, a *teacher* of the word of God, John Harvard, self-expatriated from England, as if by an express dispensation of divine Providence, came, for one short year to break the bread of life to the Church at Charlestown, and then to depart for the world of spirits, leaving his whole fortune for the foundation of a College which will bear his name in reverence and honor on the wings of Time to the end of the world.

47 In the same year in which that illustrious body sent forth the first fruits of New England education to the world, the General Court enacted a law declaring, that "For as much as the good education of children is of singular behoof and benefit to any commonwealth – that the selectmen of every town, in the several precincts and quarters where they dwell, shall have a vigilant eye over their brethren and neighbors to see, first, that none of them shall suffer so much barbarism in any of their families as not to endeavor to teach, by themselves or others, their children and apprentices, so much learning, as may enable them perfectly to read the English tongue, and knowledge of the capital laws."

48 Also that all masters of families do once a week (at the least) catechize their children and servants *in the grounds and principles of religion.*

49 There are other provisions in this law, all adapted to the purpose of carrying it into full execution.

50 Four years later (in 1646) in the enactment of a code of criminal law, it was provided, that if any child or children about sixteen years old, and of sufficient understanding, shall curse or smite their natural father or mother, he or they shall be put to death, unless it can be sufficiently testified that the parents have been very unchristianly negligent in the education of such children – and a law in the same words was some years afterwards enacted in the Plymouth Colony.

51 And in May, 1647, in addition to all these preceding enactments for the teaching of religion by the organization of Churches, and for the instruction of children in their families, a general law was passed, requiring of every township within the jurisdiction, consisting of fifty householders, to appoint forthwith, a teacher of *all* such children who should resort to him, to *write* and *read*, to be paid either by the parents or masters of such children or by the inhabitant of the town. And further, that every town

consisting of one hundred families or householders should set up a grammar school, the master thereof being able to instruct youth so far as they may be fitted for the university.

And listen to the beautiful – may I not say sublime preamble to this law, declaring the motive and purpose of its enactment. 52

> "it being one chief project of Satan to keep man from the knowledge of the Scripture, as in former times keeping them in unknown tongues, so in these latter times by persuading from the use of tongues, that so at least the true sense and meaning of the original might be clouded and corrupted with false glosses of deceivers; to the end that learning may not be buried in the graves of our forefathers, in Church and Commonwealth, the Lord assisting our endeavors. It is *therefore* ordered by this court and authority thereof," &c.

Here then, in the Laws enacted by the first settlers of New England, is a complete system of instruction, based upon the principle that human life, from the cradle to the grave, is a *school* – That at every period of his existence, man wants a *teacher*, and that his pilgrimage upon earth is but a term of childhood, in which he is to be *educated* for the manhood of a brighter world. Let the scoffer at the demure spirit and austere manner of the Puritans, survey the history of mankind – let him ransack the annals of every gathering of man into society from the confusion of Babel to the settlement of Sierra Leone, New South Wales or Liberia, and find a parallel to this primitive code of New England Colonial Law! 53

This system continued in full force until, in the progress and vicissitudes of the reformation in the parent country, the charter of the Colony was annulled by the despicable tyrant Charles the Second. Immediately after the revolution of 1688, a new Charter was obtained from William and Mary, including the Colonies of Massachusetts and Plymouth as well as the District of Maine and Nova Scotia. By the vacation of the Charter, all the preceding Colonial Laws were understood to have been superseded with it, and as the jurisdiction of the New Province extended over several preceding Colonies, which had been governed by different laws, an entire new system of Legislation became necessary. Hence, among the laws of the very first 54 sessions of the General Court under the new Charter, was an Act for the Settlement and Support of Ministers and Schoolmasters.

55 This Statute preserved and fortified the system of education which sixty years before had been established by the founders of the Colony – the system of universal education, providing at once for the support of the Pastor and the Schoolmaster, the teacher of adult age and the teacher of children, by the common contributions of all. In proportion as the population, and the worldly wealth of the Province increased, this system was expanded and enlarged by subsidiary legislation, till the revolution which severed the North American Colonies from the British Empire. At that time, when the People of the Commonwealth were called upon in their sovereign capacity to form a Constitution of Government for themselves, they declared by a special Article in their Declaration of Rights, that as the happiness of a people, and the good order and preservation of civil government, essentially depend upon piety, religion and morality, therefore the Legislature were authorized to require the several towns, parishes, precincts and other bodies politic or religious societies, to make suitable provision, at their own expense, for the institution of the public worship of God, and for the support and maintenance of public Protestant *teachers* of piety, religion and morality, in all cases where such provision shall not be made voluntarily.

56 Such was the opinion and such the ordinance of your fathers in the days of their severest trials, and when their afflictions taught them to place all their reliance upon their Creator. The people of Massachusetts in their days of prosperity and enjoyment have seen fit to repeal this Article of their Bill of Rights, and to leave the support of religion and morality, and of their teachers to the voluntary contributions of the People alone. Fondly would I hope that this constitutional alteration has proceeded from no growing indifference to the cause of piety, religion and morality, but from a firm conviction that they will be as liberally and effectively supported by voluntary contribution, as they ever have been by legislative enactment.

57 The Constitution of the Commonwealth had also a special Chapter, for the preservation, protection, and promotion of all the rights, privileges and immunities of Harvard University; and the general encouragement of Literature – making it the special duty of Legislatures and Magistrates in all future periods of the Commonwealth, to cherish the interests of literature

and the sciences, and all seminaries of them: especially the University at Cambridge, public schools, and grammar schools in towns.

From these provisions in the Constitution of the State, we have ample evidence, that at no period of our history has the interest of the People on behalf of education been more ardent and intense than it was at the time when in the midst of a most calamitous and terrible civil war, they were first summoned to exercise the rights and to wield the powers of an Independent People. 58

I have already detained you too long to protract the call upon your attention, by entering upon a detail of the legislation of the Commonwealth on the subject of education since that time. It is no pleasant recollection to bring to your minds, and it is yet a duty with which I cannot dispense, to remark that the very first act of legislation under the government of the Commonwealth, for the instruction of youth, and for the promotion of good education, presents a painful relaxation if not an inexcusable dereliction of the spirit which until then had animated all our forefathers. The act of 1693, merely repeating the provisions of that of 1647, required that every town having the number of fifty householders, or upwards, should be *constantly* provided of a schoolmaster to teach children to read and write, and that in every town of one hundred families, there should be kept a grammar school, by a person well instructed in the tongues. In the act of 1789, the duty required of towns of fifty householders is only to have schoolmasters to teach reading and writing, for such term of time shall be equivalent to six months for one school in each year. Towns of one hundred families only, were required to keep a teacher of reading and writing the year round; and only towns of two hundred families to keep a grammar school. 59

You will observe that by this alteration of the law, one-half the time of all the children of the Commonwealth, of teachable age for learning to read and write, was taken away, and the same principle as might easily be shown pervaded the whole law, diminishing the facilities for acquiring education, provided by the law, at least by one-half. What were the motives for this change I presume not now to inquire; but I cannot otherwise than consider it as evidence of an unhappy decline of that fervid spirit, for the education of children, which was so signally characteristic of the Pilgrim fathers of the Colony – of the native fathers of the Province – and of the founders of the Constitutional Commonwealth. The general spirit of your 60

laws relative to education, since that time, has been to multiply the *objects* of study upon your children, and to diminish the time which you allow them for making the acquisition of learning. This evil has not yet been removed. You may be startled at hearing that since the act of 1789, you yourselves have enjoyed facilities of learning at most half equal to those which your forefathers enjoyed from the first settlement of the Colony – and that your children now enjoy no more than you have possessed yourselves. I speak not now of private schools and academies endowed by the beneficence of individuals, or accessible to the children of opulence; but of schools provided by law, and accessible to the children of all. In very recent years, the People of the Commonwealth have kindled with a fresh ador in the cause of education, and their Legislature have shared largely of their noble enthusiasm. The annual returns of schools, from all the towns of the
61 Commonwealth; the institution of a liberal and enlightened Board of Education; the annual reports and indefatigable labors of their able and eloquent Secretary; and the provision made, by an affecting union of individual munificence with public bounty, for normal schools, to elevate the standard of instruction by the education of accomplished teachers – all these are pledges of delightful promise for the improvement of the rising and future generations.

62 But my friends and brethren of my native town, to return to the radical thought upon which I invited you to consider this subject, and which you may perhaps think more appropriate to the religious exercises of the Lord's day, and to the hallowed lips of you reverend pastor, than to the amusement of a weekday, and the discourse of a man of the world, let me close as I began intreating you to bear in mind that the invincible spirit which brought your Puritan fathers to New England, was *Education*. Let us impress it indelibly on our own minds; let us impress it to the extent of our ability upon others, that *Education* is the business of human life – that our religion is the religion of a book – and that the meaning of that book is intrusted by divine Providence to the deliberate judgement of our own understandings. That as the child must be educated for manhood upon earth, so the man must be educated upon earth, for heaven; and finally that where the foundation is not laid in Time, the superstructure cannot rise for Eternity.

Chapter 3: The Social Compact (1842)

John Quincy Adams is not the first person to write about the idea of a social compact – a mutual agreement among a people to form a government. Though at the end of the day, Adams departs from men like Locke and Rousseau, who wrote about the subject before him. For Adams, the social compact only makes sense as a historical phenomenon. Otherwise, it helps to form a government out of step both with practical reality and the demands of human nature. Throughout the essay, Adams traces America's social compact not just to the Declaration of Independence but to the formation of the many North American colonies. The result of his reflections is to create a grounded and practical basis for America's liberal democracy – one that bases our rights on the development of history instead of philosophic imaginings.

The Lecture which I propose to submit to your consideration this evening, is an examination of the principles of Democracy, of Aristocracy, and of Universal Suffrage, as exemplified in a historical review of the present Constitution of the Commonwealth of Massachusetts;[1] with some notice of the origin of human government, as maintained by the theories of divine right of Hobbes, and of Sir Robert Filmer, on one side, and by Sidney and Locke, Montesquieu and Rousseau, on the other.[2] 1

The Lecture was written more than two years since, without the slightest reference to the transactions which have since occurred in this State. — I mention this, because it might otherwise be supposed that in the delivery of the Lecture here, there is some officious interference, on my part, in the domestic concerns and dissensions of a sister State, which is far, very far, from my intention. If then there should be perceived any apparent allusion 2

1 It is perhaps worth noting that John Quincy Adams' father – John Adams – was the primary author of the Massachusetts Constitution. A document that is still largely in effect today.

2 All of these gentleman had authored their own versions of social compact theory.

to topics which have recently been much controverted in this State, the auditory will please to consider it as entirely accidental. In the Constitution of Massachusetts as originally prepared and adopted, and as subsequently amended at sundry times and in diverse manners, the people, the whole people of that Commonwealth, have always spoken for themselves. How they have so done, I propose in historical narrative to show; and if they have set the example of the gradual enlargement of the right of suffrage quietly, peaceably, without even disturbing the harmony of the community, but by the progress of public opinion ripening into universal assent, may I not humbly hope that the force of this example may operate as a lesson of wisdom, of social harmony, and of peace, beyond their territorial boundaries, and combine the most enlarged liberty for the future, with the most cordial acquiescence in the past.

3 In the preamble to the Constitution of the Commonwealth of Massachusetts, it is declared "that the body politic is formed by a voluntary association of individuals. It is a social compact, by which the whole people covenants with each citizen, and each citizen with the whole people, that all shall be governed by certain laws for the common good."

4 And by the same preamble the people of Massachusetts further declared as follows: — "We therefore, the People of Massachusetts, acknowledging with grateful hearts the goodness of the great Legislator of the Universe in affording us, in the course of his providence, an opportunity, deliberately and peaceably, without fraud, violence, or surprise, of entering into an original, explicit, and solemn compact with each other; and of forming a new Constitution of civil government for ourselves and posterity."

5 A voluntary association — a social compact — by which the whole people covenants with each citizen, and each citizen with the whole people. It would seem that human language could not be more clear and explicit, and yet there are several very important points to be settled, before we can come to a mutual understanding of its import.

6 For example; it is said that the body politic is a social compact, by which the whole people covenants with each citizen, and each citizen with the whole people. What are we to understand by the whole people?

7 The whole people of any given territory consists of all the human beings abiding upon it, men, women and children, born or in the womb, natives or foreigners, bond or free; but the word *people* itself, presupposes association - for if you suppose a million of individuals congregated on one

spot of earth ten miles square, they would not constitute a people, but by association and compact, and that association and compact must embrace them *all.*

But the whole people are not capable of contracting. 8

The children unborn or under the age of reason, are incapable of form- 9
ing any covenant. The women cannot contract separately from the men. There is a family compact preceding that which constitutes the body politic - the most sacred and solemn of all the covenants that man or woman is capable of contracting. It is only as a consequence of that compact that individuals exist, who constitute the body politic. The union of the sexes, founded in the law of nature, necessarily precedes the social compact which constitutes the body politic, which is an *association of families.*

Thus by the law of nature, the physical effect and the moral obligations 10
of the two parties to the covenant of union, are widely different. In all the stages of human society, the marriage contract confines the woman exclusively to one man; but it is believed that Christianity alone, of all human institutions, confines the man exclusively to one woman. This is one of the most excellent purifications of the law of nature, by the precepts of Christianity - entirely and exclusively favorable to the female sex, and of itself affording in the social compact an ample equivalent for the prerogative which necessarily devolves upon the man of *contracting* for her as well as for himself, and for their children under the age of ability to provide for themselves.

The woman therefore can have no direct agency in the formation 11
of the social compact which constitutes the body politic. Nor had the women of Massachusetts any direct agency in forming the Constitution of the Commonwealth. Nor are foreigners, transiently residing within the territory where the social compact is formed, parties to the body politic, albeit they are a portion of the whole people. Still less are slaves constituent parties to that covenant of the whole people with each citizen and each citizen with the whole people, albeit where slavery is tolerated they constitute an unhappy portion of the whole people subject to the government. It has indeed been repeatedly and most righteously adjudicated, by the highest judicial tribunal of Massachusetts, that slavery cannot exist within the borders of the commonwealth, under the present Constitution. There is and can be no social compact between the master and the slave.

12 Thus when in the Constitution of the Commonwealth of Massachusetts, it is said that the body politic is formed by a social compact in which the whole people covenants with each citizen and each citizen with the *whole people*, the words *whole people* in the first part of the sentence, have not the same meaning as they have in the second.

13 In the first part they mean that portion of the *people* capable of contracting for the whole and with the whole in the second, they mean the sum total of human beings bound by and included in the compact.

14 The Constitution of the State of Massachusetts was formed for themselves and their posterity, by "the people inhabiting the territory formerly called the Province of Massachusetts Bay. By the law of nature, paramount to all human compacts, that people was never for two days, for two hours, for two minutes in succession composed of the same individuals. Every minute of time, one individual passed from the number of the living to the born whence no traveler returns, and other individuals were ushered into life. The whole people therefore who formed the covenant, constituted not a tenth, perhaps not a hundredth part of the whole people bound by their obligations and entitled to their rights.

15 The covenants of the social compact must then, by the laws of nature, be made by a portion of the people for the whole - by that portion of the people capable of contracting for the whole and as the compact is formed by a *voluntary* association, not only the capacity but the *will* to contract, must concur to form the whole people who covenant with each citizen.

16 The portion of the people inhabiting the territory formerly called the Province of Massachusetts Bay, who gave their personal assent to the Constitution of the Commonwealth, was not one tenth of the whole population then inhabiting the territory.

17 And in the formation of any social compact by the *People*, we may assume it as a first principle that the individuals *covenanting* for the whole can never amount to more than one in five of the whole. These remarks may assist us in the solution of certain questions, which have recently been and are much controverted, not only within this Commonwealth, but throughout the Union, and indeed it may be said, throughout the civilized world.

18 Let us for example examine the meaning of the words Democracy and Aristocracy, with reference to the Constitution of this Commonwealth. The original meaning of the word Democracy, was, the government of the people.

It is compounded of two Greek words — "Demos," people, and "Kratos," government. The word Aristocracy, was alike compounded of the words "Aristos," best, and "Kratos," government. — The government of the best, — not the meaning at this day affixed to the word. 19

Of both these kinds of government, the earliest examples are found in the history of the Grecian republics, from whose language the names are derived. Athens was the model of the Democratic, and Sparta, of the Aristocratic republic. The Bill of Rights of the Constitution of Massachusetts, declares: 20

1. That all power resides *originally* in the *people,* and is derived from them.

2. That government is instituted for the common good; for the protection, safety, prosperity and happiness of *the people.*

3. That all elections ought to be free: and that all the inhabitants of this Commonwealth, having SUCH QUALIFICATIONS as they shall establish by their frame of government, have an equal right to elect officers, and to be elected for public employments.

4. That each individual of the society has *a right* to be protected by it, in the enjoyment of his life, liberty, and property, according to standing laws.

It is remarkable that neither the Constitution of the Commonwealth, nor the Constitution of the United States, nor the Declaration of Independence, though all issued in the name of the people, contains either of the words Democracy or Aristocracy. 21

Observe also that the institution of government is one thing, and the government itself is another. The Constitution of the Commonwealth was ordained by *the people* — that is to say, by more than two thirds of about fifteen thousand persons who voted upon it out of a population of three hundred and fifty thousand, or one vote for every thirty-five souls. 22

Under this Constitution, the government of the Commonwealth of Massachusetts is a government of the *people,* - by their representatives. Is it a democracy? certainly not in the acceptance of the word as it was originally understood — certainly not as Athens was a democracy. But in whatever sense you use the word democracy, for the institution or administration of government, the people exercising power are and can be only a portion, and a very small portion of the whole people over whom power is exercised. Government is the exercise of power directing or controlling the will of 23 human beings. This power may be exercised by every individual over him or herself, or it may be exercised by one or more individuals over others.

24 Of all governments upon earth, the most important, and perhaps the most difficult, is self government - and as self love and social are the same, if this self government were possessed in perfection by the whole human race, no other government would be needed or could exist.

25 But perfect self government is not allotted to man upon earth. There is a law of nature, or in more proper words, a law of God, the author of nature, subjected to which the human being comes into life, and from the power of which he can be released only by death. By this law of God, the human being comes into life, the child of two parents, male and female, both of one species, but of different constitutions, adapted to each other for union, but subject to different modifications of the law of nature, and of course to different applications of the principle of self government.

26 The child comes into life utterly incapable, not only of self government, but of self preservation. Left to itself, it must perish at the hour of its birth. For its preservation, the first want of its nature is food, and the same nature which has given the appetite, points for its supply to the fountain of life, the maternal breast.

27 We must not forget that the child comes into life, produced by the union of two parents many months before; that each of these parents, many years before, had been by a similar union of their parents, brought into life in the same manner, and that thus in the search for the laws of self government we must ascend to one couple of human beings, created, not born, the primitive parents of the whole human race. The holy scriptures inform us historically that such was the fact, and if there be in this auditory, a philosopher who disbelieves the scriptural account of the creation, and yet seeks for the origin and sources of human government and human freedom, let him give us *his account* of the origin and present existence of the human race.

28 But whatever that origin may have been, to the continued existence of the race through successive generations, four individuals, two of each sex, are indispensable bearing to each other the respective relations of husband and wife, father and mother - son and daughter, brother and sister.

29 Man is therefore by the law of nature's God, a *social being*. He cannot exist alone. He cannot be born, but by the union of two individuals of his

own species and of different sex. He cannot continue the species but by the co-operation of another individual of a sex different from his own.

The nuptial union then is by the law of nature, the foundation of 30
human society, and it necessarily superinduces to the law of self government, the law of family government - for each of these four individuals has selfish passions which must be governed, some of which are in harmony with those of the other three, and others discordant with those of one or more of the rest. The conjugal, parental, filial and fraternal relations exist between them, and originate between them rights and duties to the enjoyment and obligation of which, self government is not adequate. There must be a common government, subject to the control of one will, and this constitutes the law of family government.

This government is, in its nature complicated. It is not despotic, nor 31
even absolute. The conjugal authority is more limited than the parental. The authority of the husband and wife is reciprocal — the paternal and maternal authority over the children is not the same. For years from the time of its birth, the child, incapable of self government, is committed by nature to the government of the mother — but that government itself is controlled and modified by the preceding nuptial bond between the father and mother, and the law of that union gives to the father the government of the family.

In the scriptural account of the Creation, it is related that the woman 32
was created as an helpmeet for the man. His authority over her was not given to him in the state of innocence, but as a penalty upon her disobedience to the divine command. The exercise of the power of family government was thus expressly conferred upon the man, and entailed upon their posterity till the final redemption of the race, while the sentence upon the man for hearkening unto the voice of his wife, in disobedience and violation of the condition upon which he had been placed in the Garden of Eden, was, that he should till the ground and eat bread in the sweat of his face, till he should return to the dust out of which he had been taken.

Now, then, the *social compact* which constitutes the *body politic*, as 33
defined in the preamble to the Constitution of the Commonwealth, is formed by an association, not merely of individuals, but of families; and although the covenant is, as it is declared to be, between each citizen and the whole people, yet the actual pledge of each family is given only by its *father*, who stands sponsor for his wife, for all his unmarried daughters,

for his sons under age, and for all his posterity, while the compact remains unchanged. So it was that the Constitution of this Commonwealth was formed. It was the work of the whole people; but no woman, no man under the age of twenty-one years, had a hand either in its preparation, or in the final vote by which it was adopted.

34 When the government is once constituted, the action of the people upon its operations is confined to the mere process of election, and the concurrence of popular opinion and feeling. The Bill of Rights of Massachusetts declares that all elections ought to be *free*; and that all the inhabitants, *having such qualifications as they shall establish by their frame of government*, have an equal right to elect officers, and to be elected to public employments.

35 By this article, the right of voting at elections, and of being elected to office, is confined to the individuals having the *qualifications* established by the Constitution.

36 The qualifications established by the Constitution of 1780, were for the right of voting: 1. Sex, confined to males. 2. Age, twenty-one years. 3. Place and time, inhabitancy for one year next preceding the election. 4. Property, a freehold estate within the Commonwealth, of the annual income of three pounds, or ten dollars, or any estate of the value of sixty pounds, or two hundred dollars.

37 The qualifications for election, as a member of the House of Representatives, were, sex and age, as for the voters — choice by written votes - inhabitancy for at least a year preceding the election, - a freehold within the town, of one hundred pounds value, or ratable estate to the value of two hundred pounds: — as a Senator, a freehold estate, within the Commonwealth, of the value of three hundred pounds at least, or personal estate to the value of six hundred pounds, or both to the amount of the same sum - inhabitancy within the Commonwealth for five years immediately preceding the election, and in the district for which he is chosen, at the time of election; - as Governor, or Lieutenant Governor - inhabitancy within the Commonwealth, for seven years next preceding the election; a freehold estate, within the Commonwealth, of the value of one thousand pounds — and that he should declare himself to be of the *Christian* religion.

38 The declaration upon oath in the belief of the truth of the Christian religion was also required of all Councilors, Senators, Representatives, and Executive and Judicial officers, but not for the exercise of the right of voting.

This Constitution was made and adopted by the *people* of Massachu- 39
setts in the year 1780. It was the work of the democracy — that is, of the whole people; but there is no definition of democracy, which can claim it as embraced within its principles. There was a provision in the same Constitution for the assembly of a Convention, for the revisal and amendment of it, at the end of fifteen years, if desired by two thirds of the qualified voters throughout the Commonwealth. In the year 1795, this question was submitted to the people; but they were so well satisfied with the operation of the system after fifteen years of experience, that they declined by a large majority the calling of a Convention.

A longer experience of forty years had however produced a change of 40
public opinion in the generation succeeding that which had formed the original Constitution. — In 1820, a Convention was assembled, containing a full representation of all that remained of the people of Massachusetts Bay, for immediately before this event, the Commonwealth of Massachusetts had been severed in two. The largest portion of its territory, and the most thriving portion of its population had been set off, by common consent, as a separate State, reducing the Commonwealth in extent and power, from one of the largest, to one of the smallest in the Union.

At the Convention of 1820, nine amendments to the Constitution of 41
1780 were prepared and recommended to the people, by whom they were adopted on the ninth of April, 1821.

By the last of these amendments, it was provided that if, at any time 42
thereafter, any specific and particular amendment to the Constitution should be proposed in the General Court, and agreed to by a majority of the Senators, and two thirds of the members of the House of Representatives present and voting thereon, such proposed amendment or amendments, should be entered on the journals of the two houses, with the yeas and nays taken thereon, and referred to the General Court, then next to be chosen, and should be published — and if in the General Court next chosen as aforesaid, such proposed amendment or amendments shall be agreed to by a majority of the Senators and two thirds of the members of the House of Representatives present and voting thereon; then it shall be the duty of the General Court to submit such proposed amendment or amendments to the people; and if they shall be approved and ratified by a majority of the qualified voters voting thereon, at meetings legally warned

and holden for that purpose, they shall become part of the Constitution of this Commonwealth.

43 Since the Convention of 1820, three additional amendments have been engrafted upon the Constitution — the first in 1831, the second in 1833, and the third in the year 1840. We are now prepared to affix a precise and definite idea to the fundamental principle asserted in the fifth article of our Declaration of Rights, that all power resides originally in *the people*, and is derived from them — and to observe how this power has been practically exercised by the people of this Commonwealth in the formation and successive amendments of their Constitution.

44 We see that from the first step to the last of this process, the people exercising power is, as by the laws of nature it must be, only a portion of the people over whom power is exercised; the latter embracing every human being within the territory, the former consisting only of *qualified voters.*

45 The Convention which prepared the Constitution of 1780 was assembled by the authority of a preceding representative Assembly, revolutionary in its character, and itself elected by *qualified* voters. The members of the constituent Convention were elected by qualified voters. The Constitution when sent out to the people, was adopted and ratified by *qualified* voters; and the Convention declared it to be the Constitution of the Commonwealth, because it appeared, by the returns, that more than two thirds of the voters upon it had approved it.

46 It is said, by Rousseau, that the social compact can be formed only by *unanimous* consent, because the rule itself, that a majority of votes shall prevail, can only be established by agreement, that is, by compact. But I have endeavored to show, you will judge with what success, that the social compact, constituting the body politic, is, and by the law of nature must be, a compact, not merely of individuals, but of families, — that the civil association necessarily presupposes a family compact, constituting a community, for the whole of which there can be but one vote. We read, indeed, in ancient history, of a republic of Amazons, consisting entirely of women; but if we are to believe the accounts which we have of them, their constituent compact was not very *social*, nor was it at all founded upon the laws of nature, or the *rights of man.*

47 One of their fundamental laws was to murder their own male children. Another, to amputate one of the breasts of their daughters. If such a *body politic* ever existed, it was doubtless extinguished by the alliance of their

Queen Thalestris with Alexander of Macedon, and the consequent subjugation of the female republic to the conqueror of the world.

There have been, in more modern times, and even under the Christian dispensation, communities exclusively composed of men, and others of women. They have been sometimes invested with sovereign powers, and the law of celibacy has been imposed upon their rulers, but not upon the people subject to their sway. They have served rather as warnings than as examples to mankind; they may have constituted bodies politic, but can never be considered as a people, from whom was derived the power exercised by their government over them. The power exercised by the government of the Commonwealth of Massachusetts over the whole people, that is over every human being within the state, was conferred by a majority, amounting to more than two thirds of the actually voting qualified voters. 48

This is not Democracy as understood in the theories of modern times. We are told that Democracy is the government of the whole people, and that universal suffrage is its only rule - that the democracy of numbers constitutes the sovereign power, and that it must always be governed by majorities. 49

But Democracy is not, and cannot be, the government merely of numbers. The social compact which constitutes a sovereign state is a compact not only of individuals, but of families. The people who form the Constitution and administer the government, are, and can be, only a portion of the people governed by it. No compact can be made by persons incapable of contracting; and as the family union must, in the order of nature, precede the compact which constitutes the body politic, and as by the law of nature and of God, the family must be governed by one will, that of the father, Democracy is not, never was, never can be, the government merely of numbers. 50

The body politic consists of human beings, male and female - of adults and children. In its formation, the father alone is qualified to vote for himself, for the wife, the mother, and the infant children. The vote, by the law of nature and of God, must be confined to the male sex, because the contract, embracing the whole family, one member of the family must pledge the faith, and stipulate for the rights of the whole. That member is the husband and father. The wife is not qualified to vote, because, by the nuptial tie and the law of God, her will has been subjected to that of her husband — because, were it otherwise, the vote of the husband and of 51 the wife might be opposed to and would annul each other, and either the body politic could not be formed, or it must be formed without the vote or consent of every family thus divided. Here then are *qualifications* to vote in the formation of the body politic prescribed by the laws of nature and of God, which must limit the law of universal suffrage, and cannot be overcome. The husband and wife cannot both vote, because their votes, like opposite forces in nature, would destroy each other, and neither would be a party to the compact. This disqualification is permanent and irremovable.

52 That of the children is temporary. The capacity to contract is confined to the age of discretion. That is different in different individuals; and the capacity to contract depends, in some degree, upon the nature of the contract itself. The capacity to form the nuptial contract, comes with the age of puberty, differing in different climates, and of earlier maturity for the woman than for the man.

53 The capacity for voting at the formation of the body politic, may be reasonably fixed at that period of life, when the youth, emancipated from the parental authority, goes forth into the world to provide for his own subsistence. This age, by the original Constitution of Massachusetts, was fixed at twenty-one years. And so it continues to this day, with one exception. In the 5th article of amendment to the Constitution, adopted in April, 1821, it is provided, that "in the elections of captains and subalterns of the militia, all the members of their respective companies, as well those under, as those above the age of twenty-one years, shall have a right to vote." The reason for this variation from the general rule of qualification for voting, is that eighteen years is the age at which the citizen is enrolled for service in the militia; and when the community calls upon the individual for military service which may involve the sacrifice of his life, it is but just that he should at the same time be invested with the right of voting for the officers by whom he is to be commanded.

54 But much more extensive alterations of the qualifications, as well of the voters as of the officers of the Commonwealth, were established by the amendments recommended by the Convention of 1820, and adopted in April, 1821. The qualifications of *property* and of *belief in the truth of the Christian Religion* were abolished. Instead of the qualification for the right to vote, of a freehold estate within the town of the voter's residence, of the annual income of ten dollars, or any estate of the value of two hundred dollars, the qualification substituted, and now established, is the previous

payment, by the voter himself, or by his parent, master, or guardian, of any state, or county tax, within two years next preceding the election, assessed upon him in any town or district of the Commonwealth. The qualification of one year's residence in the town where the vote is cast is superseded, and one year's residence in the Commonwealth, and six calendar months in the town, next preceding the election, is substituted. Paupers and persons under guardianship are expressly excluded from the right of voting by the amendment, who had not been by the original Constitution.

The qualification of previous payment of a tax, with the express exclu- 55
sion of paupers, differs perhaps not much in practical operation from that of property prescribed by the original Constitution, but the protection and security of property is not less the purpose of the social compact than that of persons.

And although several of the amendments to the original Constitu- 56
tion of Massachusetts have greatly diminished the representation of property, and enlarged that of persons in the Legislature, there still remains an overpowering representation of property, in the Legislature of the Union, though exclusively confined by the Constitution of the United States to the southern section of the country.

The philosophical examination of the foundations of civil society, of 57
human governments, and of the rights and duties of men, is among the consequences of the Protestant Reformation. Under the hierarchy of the church of Rome, human government was of divine institution. The powers that be, were ordained of God; and the monarch, at the head of the nation, was the Lord's anointed. The principle of the Protestant Reformation was, to deny, not that human government was of divine institution, but that implicit belief and obedience was due to the commandments of men. The controversy was at first confined to the extent and limitations of human authority in matters of religion. The Roman Pontiffs claimed the right, and had exercised the power, of granting indulgences for the commission of sins, and these indulgences were actually sold for money. This monstrous pretension, striking, in the name of religion, at the root of all morality, was too much for the human mind to endure. Martin Luther, an Augustine monk, a professor at a German University, there set up the standard of human freedom, and denied the *right* of the Bishop of Rome to grant indulgences for the commission of sins. Simple as this proposition now appears to you, vital as it is to the freedom and the virtue of the human

race, more than three centuries have passed away since it was proclaimed by an obscure monk at the University of Wittenberg. Some of the bloodiest and most desolating wars that ever afflicted the human race have been waged to maintain it, and now at the end of three hundred and twenty-five years, it is yet denied by more than half the nations of Christendom.

58 The question raised by Martin Luther, involved the whole theory of the *rights* of individual man, paramount to all human authority. The sale of indulgences was but one of an enormous mass of usurpations, which the pretended successors of Peter, the fisherman of Galilee, had for a series of ages been heaping upon the back of the Christian world, till it was sinking under its load of oppression.

59 The reformation of Luther raised the question of *right* between the subject and the sovereign. Its first application was only to ecclesiastical power - to the authority of the Bishops of Rome. But the question of individual right being once raised, and successfully maintained, could not but, in process of time, be applied as well to political as to ecclesiastical authority. Divine right was no longer a sufficient commission for kings to reign, and princes to decree justice.

60 In Germany, the controversy was confined to the extent and limitations of ecclesiastical power. In France, the progress of the reformation was arrested by the apostacy of Henry of Navarre. From the cell of an Augustine monk and the hall of a German University, issued forth the freedom of the soul from spiritual tyranny. From Saint Stephen's Chapel and the electric spark from mind to mind in an English House of Commons, went forth civil and political freedom, to penetrate into the prison where the body of man was confined, and to lead him forth to the light of day, as the angel of the Lord in a blaze of supernatural light raised up Peter in the dungeon of Herod, smote him on the side, while the chains fell off from his hands, and led him out to preach to the nations the blessed gospel of peace and love.

61 The kings and queens of England arrested the progress of the reformation, by transferring to themselves the supremacy, which they extorted from the bishops of Rome. But the talisman of *human rights* dissolved the spell of political as well as of Ecclesiastical power. The Calvinists of Geneva and the Puritans of England, contested the right of kings to prescribe articles of faith to their people, right and this question necessarily drew after it the general question of the origin of all human government. This question gave rise to the civil wars of the seventeenth century in England,

and to the two parties of Royalists and Republicans, or of Cavaliers and Roundheads. In search of the principle of human government, Hobbes, a royalist, assumed that the state of nature between man and man was a state of war - whence it followed that government originated in *conquest.* Upon this, Rousseau justly remarks, that a people subjected by the right of conquest, are perfectly right in submitting to the government, as long as they cannot help themselves; but that submission is not peace, and that the first moment of power to resist, confers upon them the right to cast off the yoke. The theory of Hobbes is directly opposite to that of Jesus Christ. It severs the Gordian knot with the sword, extinguishes all the rights of man, and makes force the corner stone of all human government. It is the only theory upon which slavery can be justified as conformable to the law of nature. This is Sir John Falstaff's law, when speaking of Justice Shallow, he says, if the young dace be a bait for the old pike, I see no reason in the *law of nature* why I may not snap at *him.*[3]

Sir Robert Filmer,[4] by a theory far more plausible though not more 62
sound than that of Hobbes, derived the origin of human government from the scriptures of the Old Testament — from the grant of the earth to Adam, and afterwards to Noah. Perceiving that government, by the law of nature, must embrace an association of families as well as of individuals, he inferred that from the absolute authority conferred by nature to parents over their infant children, the power of the government over nations was identical with that of the patriarchs over their descendants, absolute and unlimited.

I say that this theory was *plausible*. It is true, as in this discourse I have 63
endeavored to demonstrate, that by the nature of man and the laws of God, the social compact which constitutes the body politic, or in other words the sovereign state, must be formed by an association of families, as well as of individuals; — that the government of each family, as a community, must be regulated by one will — that of the father — and that God did by *covenant* give the renovated earth to Noah and his *family*, and the land of Canaan, with the promise of blessings to be shared by *all* the *families* of the earth, to Abraham and *his seed*; a promise, the accomplishment of

3 Adams is referring to the Shakespeare character Sir John Falstaff who, though a bumbling buffoon, argues that justice is essentially the triumph of the strong over the weak.

4 Sir Robert Filmer was a British political philosopher born in 1588 whose published works argued strongly in favor of the divine right of kings to rule their people.

which was not to *commence*, till after the lapse of many generations, and which cannot be consummated till after the lapse of many more. But the vital error of Filmer was in assuming that the natural authority of the father over the child was either permanent or unlimited, and still more that the authority of the husband over the wife was unlimited. Sir Robert Filmer did not perceive, that, by the laws of nature and of God, every individual human being is born with *rights*, which no other individual or combination of individuals can take away. That *all* exercise of human authority must be under the limitation of right and wrong, and that all despotic power over human beings is exercised in *defiance* of the laws of nature and of God - all Sir John Falstaff's law of nature between the young dace and the old pike. The authority of the husband over the wife is itself the result of a *compact* preceding in its nature that of the body politic. The union of the sexes is necessary for the preservation and continuance of the species, but this union in every individual case, must be formed by mutual consent, and without exercise of authority on either side. Its only law, is the law of love; and

"Love, free as air, at sight of human ties,
Spreads his light wings and in a moment flies."[5]

64 The nuptial tie of nature then must be formed by mutual *consent*, but its permanency must be by the mutual pledge of faith, that is by covenant or compact. Now the terms of that compact may be varied at the discretion of the parties in every single case, but there is one incident necessary to them all — the concerns common to both parties must be regulated by one will. It may be the will of the husband, or of the wife, or alternately of either. By the law of nature the woman must bear the child, and the parental authority first devolves upon her. But by another law of nature, the union itself has originated in the *will* of the husband. The first advances must be made by him.

"She, as a veil, down to the slender waist
Her unadorned golden tresses wore
Dishevell'd, but in wanton ringlets wav'd
As the vine curls her tendrils, which *implied*

5 A line taken from Alexander Pope's poem, "Eloisa to Abelard."

> Subjection, but required with gentle sway,
> And by her yielded, by him best received.
> Yielded with coy submission, modest pride,
> And sweet, reluctant, amorous delay."[6]

65 The will of the husband then is by the law of nature the origin of the marriage contract, of its permanent continuance and of its last results, and when the family come to form with others the social compact and the body politic, that will of the husband and father must speak for the whole family, that is the wife and infant children. But this is surely neither unlimited nor even absolute authority. It is limited by the natural, inalienable rights both of the wife and of the children. The patriarchal origin of government therefore confers no despotic power, and the theory of Sir Robert Filmer, falls by the law of nature to the ground.

66 The history of Filmer's work is remarkable. It was composed and published in the heat of the struggle between King Charles the first and the Commons of England, which terminated in the overthrow of the monarchy and the death of King Charles upon the scaffold.[7] It was the theory of government upon which the *cause* of the house of Stuart was sustained. No one can be surprised that such a cause was swept away by a moral and political whirlwind that carried with it all the institutions of civil society, so that its march was a wild desolation. Charles was brought to the block—his family were hunted like wild beasts, escaping almost as by miracle into banishment, to live twelve years in such abject poverty, that his widow, the daughter of Henry the Fourth, of France, was compelled to keep her bed from day to day, in the winter's cold of Paris, for want of fuel to warm the chamber in which she lived. After twelve years of proscription and of wretchedness, the Stuarts were restored to the throne of England, by a counter whirlwind as sweeping as that by which they had been expelled. During the interregnum, while the long Parliament had reigned in the name of Democracy and Cromwell, by the sword of Naseby[8] and by visions of regenerating grace, Filmer had died, and his book had fallen into oblivion.

---

6 From John Milton's *Paradise Lost.* Book 4, Lines 304-311.

7 Adams is here referring to the English Civil War that temporarily saw the fall of the British monarchy.

8 The Battle of Naseby was the decisive battle that ended all real hope of a royalist victory over parliamentary forces in the English Civil War.

67 In the first years after the Restoration, there was little speculation upon the nature of government. The reformers in church and state had made their own government so universally detested, and the name even of a republic so odious, that the reigns of Charles the second, and of his brother James, are among the most tyrannical and oppressive in English history. Charles was a dissolute, witty and profligate sensualist - James a gloomy and fanatical bigot. Charles corrupted the morals of the nation by his personal vices — degraded the honors of the constitutional aristocracy by heaping them upon prostitutes, and bastardized with spurious blood the whole peerage of the realm. James, by falling back into the arms of the Church of Rome, vainly struggled to turn back the tide of religious reformation, and the divine right of kings, and passive obedience, and non-resistance, became the only theories of government which could save the neck of an Englishman from the axe of an executioner. It was at this period that the book of Sir Robert Filmer was dug up from the grave in which it had slumbered with him, and became the Bible of the Stuarts and their train. Sir Robert Filmer's Patriarcha, was republished in 1680, towards the close of the life and reign of Charles the second, and again in 1685, the first year of the reign of the second James. The republican spirit of the Anglo Saxon[9] had slumbered on the white cliffs of Albion, and in his sleep, like the man-mountain in Lilliput[10], had been pinned down to the earth by the threads of a spider's web for cords. On the first re-appearance of Filmer's book he awoke, and like the strong man of Israel, at the cost of his own life, shook down the Temple of Dagon, and buried himself and the Philistines together under its ruins.[11]

68 Sidney's Discourses on Government were written for the express and avowed purpose of refuting the doctrines of Filmer, who had been forty years dead. Sidney, a son of the Earl of Leicester, allied by the female line, to the Northumberland Percys, was born of the noblest blood of England. Born in 1622, he came into active life precisely at the agony of the conflict

9 By referencing the "republican spirit of the Anglo-Saxon," Adams is making use of a theory common at the time that stated the Anglo-Saxon tribes brought free government from their forests in Germany.

10 The Kingdom of Lilliput is a fictional land inhabited by minuscule people in Jonathan Swift's *Gulliver's Travels*.

11 This reference refers to First Samuel, in which the Philistines are said to worship the god Dagon, whose Temple is destroyed repeatedly after the Ark of the Covenant is stolen from the Jewish people.

between the Democracy and the Monarchy of England. He took his side not so much *for* the cause of the Parliament, as *against* that of the king. Though under twenty-six years of age, he was appointed one of the Judges on the trial of Charles, but he thirsted not for blood, and took no part in that cruel mockery of justice. His cause was *Liberty*, and the anarchy of the Rump and the bayonets of Cromwell, were as little to his taste as the crosier of Laud, or the patriarchal sceptre of Filmer.[12] After the abdication of Richard Cromwell, in 1659, Sidney was appointed a member of the Council of State, and immediately after was sent with two other commissioners, to mediate a peace between Denmark and Sweden. This they accomplished, but in the mean time the Stuarts were restored, and Charles was extinguishing as he vainly imagined, in the blood of the regicides, all future opposition to the divine right of kings. Sidney, though not included in the number of the regicides, was one of the main pillars of the republican cause, and was personally obnoxious to Charles the second, for some occasional offensive remarks that he had recently made - especially for two Latin lines that he had written in the album of the royal library at Copenhagen:

69

"Manus haec inimica tyrannis
Ense petit placidam sub libertate quietam."

"This hand, the rule of tyrants to oppose
Seeks with the sword fair freedom's soft repose."

The second of which lines, "Ense petit placidam sub libertate quie- 70
tam" — was adopted by the founders of the Commonwealth of Massachusetts, as the motto to the arms of the State; - a motto lasting as the Commonwealth herself, and ever admonishing her sons that the enjoyment of quiet freedom is the *only* lawful motive for drawing the sword to shed blood in resistance to tyranny, and signally marking at the same time their approbation of this sublime sentiment and their profound veneration for the character of Algernon Sidney. He was advised by his father and other friends not to return to England, and led a wandering life, residing from time to time in various parts of Europe, for seventeen years, till

12 The Rump Parliament and Cromwell supported a despotic sort of republican government, while William Laud was the Bishop of Canterbury who backed the centralizing monarchy of Charles I.

after narrowly escaping assassination by ten men sent by Charles as emissaries into Germany for that express purpose, he obtained in 1677, by the intervention of Henry Saville, then ambassador of Charles, at the Court of France, and afterwards Earl and Marquis of Halifax, a pardon, and returned to England. Three years after, appeared the first republication of Filmer's Patriarcha, upon which Sidney composed his Discourses on Government, which however he never published.

71 The work was yet unfinished, when in 1683, he was arrested, tried and executed for treason, by participation in what is called the Rye House plot. There was but one witness, the infamous Lord Howard, upon the fact but instead of witnesses, extracts from these Discourses concerning government, these speculations upon the natural rights of man, were brought up as evidence of treason against him. They were not even proved but by a mere comparison with other papers, to be his hand writing. He died a martyr to that *old cause* in which he had from his youth been engaged.

72 The Discourses concerning Government, at once demolished and immortalized the work of Filmer. His name and his book are now remembered only to be detested. But the first principles of morals and politics which have long been settled, acquire the authority of self evident truths, which, when first discussed, may have been vehemently and pertinaciously contested. That the doctrines of Filmer had taken deep root and obstinate hold of the English mind, is evident, not only from historical testimony; not only from this great work of Sidney itself, but from the exertions of a kindred soul, John Locke, who seven years after the death of Sidney, and two years after the practical operation of the patriarchal theory had been illustrated by what was called the abdication of James the second, published ten elaborate treatises on government, in the first of which, says their title page, "the false principles and foundation of Sir Robert Filmer and his followers are *detected* and overthrown;" and the second was an Essay concerning the true original extent and end of Civil Government. The principles of Sidney and of Locke, constitute the foundation of the North American Declaration of Independence, and together with the subsequent writings of Montesquieu and Rousseau, that of the Constitution of the Commonwealth of Massachusetts, and of the Constitution of the United States.

73 Under these two Constitutions we live; and our allegiance is due, by the one to this great confederated Union; by the other, to our beloved Commonwealth. Neither of these Constitutions separately, nor the two

in combined harmony, can without a gross and fraudulent perversion of language, be termed a Democracy. They are neither Democracy, Aristocracy, nor Monarchy. They form together a mixed Government, compounded not only of the three elements of Democracy, Aristocracy, and Monarchy, but with a fourth added element of Confederacy. We are then as Mr. Jefferson forty years ago said, all federalists - all republicans — but not all *Democrats*, no more than we are all Aristocrats or Monarchists.

We are divided into parties - warm and bitter parties, which are not 74
necessarily, but are very apt to degenerate into factions. One of the properties common to all parties, and symptomatic of a tendency to degenerate into faction, is the assumption to themselves, of a popular name, and branding their adversaries with an odious one. It sometimes happens that antagonist parties both assume the same name because it is popular, and stigmatize their adversaries with another name because it is odious. This has been and it is feared will continue to be the practice of all our parties. The struggle was long and acrimonious for the name of Republicans, assumed by both parties but claimed as exclusive by one of them; and when Mr. Jefferson had settled that *all* were Republicans, his own party dissatisfied with the decision, cast off the appellation for which they had so steadily contended, and called themselves *Democrats*.[13] The Constitution of the United States, when adopted by the people of the United States, was so far from being considered as a Democracy, that Patrick Henry charged it in the Virginia Convention, with an awful squinting towards Monarchy. The tenth number of the Federalist, written by James Madison, is an elaborate and unanswerable essay upon the vital, and radical difference between a Democracy and a Republic. - But it is impossible entirely to disconnect the relation between names and things; when the anti-federal party dropped the name of Republicans to assume that of *Democrats*, their principles underwent a corresponding metamorphosis, and they are now the most devoted and most obsequious champions of executive power, — the very life guards of the Commander in Chief of the armies and navies of the Union.

But they have assumed the name of Democrats, and they tell us that 75
Democracy is the dominion of man over his accidents — or that Democracy

13 The self-styled Democratic party emerged in the early years of John Quincy Adams' presidency and by this time had become the most dominant political force in America. Founded on Jacksonian populism it pushed for more egalitarian political institutions, westward expansion, and a powerful chief executive.

is the government of the *whole* people and nothing but the people; that no fraction of the people, not the purest, not the strongest, not the wealthiest, not the wisest, no — the whole people, man, woman, child, born or unborn, foreigner and native the lunatic, the lover and the poet, all, all must govern and that is Democracy — that is *eternal justice ruling through the people.*

76 But the *name* of *Democracy* it has been discovered is very TAKING among the multitude, because, after all, it is but the investment of the *multitude* with absolute power.

77 Were I permitted to select a name for the party to which I should wish to belong, it would be that of Constitutionalist; meaning thereby faithful adhesion to the two Constitutions, of the United States and of the Commonwealth. They are the fruits of the wisdom and valour of our forefathers matured and modified by the experience of more than three-score years. They are both the work of the people; one of the Union, — the other of the State - not of the whole people, by the phantom of universal suffrage, but of the whole people by that portion of them capable of contracting for the whole. The work, not of eternal justice ruling through the people, but of man, - frail, fallen, imperfect man, following the dictates of his nature and aspiring to perfection. It is not Democracy, - nor Aristocracy, nor Monarchy, but a compound of them all, of which Democracy is the oxygen or vital air, too pure in itself for human respiration, but which, in the union with other elements equally destructive in themselves and less pure, forms that moral and political atmospheric air, in which we live and move and have our being.

78 But after and above all, let us never forget, in the most fervent heat of our party conflicts, that there is a *cause*, embracing and transcending all others — like the all surrounding orb in the philosophical theory of the learned and ingenious Bowdoin, President of the Convention which formed the Constitution of our Commonwealth, which he supposed necessary as a counterbalance to the principle of gravitation, to preserve the system of the material universe from ruin — that cause, before which all party spirit must hide its diminished head - kindling every affection of the heart, and inspiring every faculty of the soul - the cause of *our Country.*

Chapter 4: On Astronomy (1843)

At first blush this essay – originally delivered at the opening of a government funded observatory in Cincinnati Ohio – seems like a dull history of the science of astronomy. Certainly, Adams spends a great deal of the following pages both extolling the virtues of star gazing and describing in detail the development of the field over the centuries. However, baked into the essay is a broader defense of general education. In Adams' time, as in ours, many Americans openly disdained any field of study without obvious real-life application. Adams took a very different approach; throughout this essay he argues that all education helps to bring humans closer to perfection. The study of the heavens, no less than religion or mechanical engineering, is a vital part of a life well lived.

Fellow Citizens of the Astronomical Society of Cincinnati, Fellow Citizens, 1
Ladies and Gentlemen:

When the people of thirteen colonies separately chartered by a succes- 2
sion of English kings, on a portion of the continent of North America, united to assume to themselves the transcendent powers of sovereignty, and to declare the ties of their allegiance to their sovereign beyond the seas, forever dissolved, they appealed for their justification in the performance of an act, which, without that resort would have been a crime of the deepest dye that can be committed by human hands, Treason against their country, to the Supreme judge of the world, and to the primitive rights bestowed by Him upon them and upon all mankind, by the laws of nature, antecedent and paramount to all human association, or human government They appealed to their rights as men, and they declared that they held those rights to be self-evident truths That they held them in common with all mankind; because all men were born equal That bestowed as they were by God, their creator, they never could be divested of them, even by themselves, and much less could they be wrested from them, by the might of others. That unless forfeited by his own wrong every individual of

the human race comes into being, endowed with those rights, and that if the whole compass of human power could be concentrated in one arm, it would be impotent to take away, however it might ravish or prostrate those rights personified in the meanest individual of the breed of man, crawling upon the face of the earth.

3 What an exalted and sublime idea of the character of man! How must our nature swell with pride, at the consciousness of being members of a community by the fundamental principles of which, every soul belonging to it, is born to the inheritance of freedom; Born with rights which he may forfeit by his own wrong, but otherwise inaccessible to human power! Government had never before been explicitly declared to be based on this foundation. Governments had by the people of England been declared to be founded on a compact between the sovereign and the people, and they had been classified as monarchies, aristocracies, or democracies, all of which had been said to be liable to degenerate: the monarchy into tyranny, the aristocracy into oligarchy, and the democracy into ochlocracy or the government of a lawless multitude. But it was admitted on all sides, by the votaries of each of the three simple forms, that government once instituted must necessarily be absolute and unlimited. And although the existence of primitive rights belonging to man at his birth, was admitted, it was asserted, that by entering into the social compact, man surrendered all his rights, and took in return, such as the ruling power was pleased to bestow upon him. The Declaration of Independence acknowledges no such principle. It recognizes no despotism, monarchical, aristocratic or democratic. It declares individual man, born with rights, of which, while blamelessly possessed, no government can deprive him. But by the very nature of the grant, the right can be possessed, only upon the condition, of respecting the same rights in all other men. The laws of nature and of nature's God therefore are laws of duty, as well as laws of right. Nature says to every individual man, your rights are all held by the tenure of reverence for the same rights, in all other men. If you infringe the right of any other man, you place yourself at war with your brother, and in assailing any one of his rights, you make him the master of your own.

4 The natural equality of mankind, is thus the parent of universal freedom. It follows irresistibly, from the fact, that man is at once a rational and a social being. His reason is given him by his Creator to govern his conduct through life, and he can neither be deprived of it by violence, nor can he

transfer it to another. And hence the rights derived from it, are declared to be inalienable.

There is a point of view, from which this new modeling of the institu- 5
tion of civil society, is to be considered, with reference to the special subject upon which I have been honored with your invitation at this time to address you. The intuitive genius of Shakespeare, which made the creative imaginations of the drama, the vehicle of inspiration to the noblest maxims, and the sublimest principles of morals, has said, in one of his immortal conceptions:

"Nature never lends
The smallest parcel of her excellence,
But like a thrifty goddess she determines
Herself the glory of a creditor -
Both thanks - and use."[1]

The license of poetry, substitutes the name of Nature, as the hand 6
maid of the omnipotent Creator of the worlds, and allows her to pre-scribe the conditions, and to exact the returns to the bounties which he bestows upon the creatures of his hands. It is God, the grants of whose favor, are instruments of beneficent power, and who in imparting them to his rational offspring, exacts the twofold return of thanks, and use. And thus the acknowledgment of the unalienable right of man to life, liberty and the pursuit of happiness, is at the same time an acknowledgment of the omnipotence, the omniscience and the all-pervading goodness of God. Man thus endowed, is a being of loftier port, of larger dimensions, of infinitely increased and multiplied powers, and of heavier and deeper responsibilities, than man invested with no such attributes or capacities. If then it be true, that man is born with unalienable rights, among which are life, liberty and the pursuit of happiness, it is equally true, that he is born under the deepest and most indispensable duties of ceaseless gratitude to his Maker, for the grant of these endowments, and of exercising, maintaining and supporting them, by all the faculties, Unintellectual and physical, with which he has been provided to that end. Nor is the duty less peremptory and irremissible,

1 This is a quote derived from William Shakespeare's play *Measure for Measure.* It is spoken by Duke Vincentio to Escalus.

of holding and enjoying these rights, with the inviolate respect and observance of the same rights in others.

7 Man is a social and a rational being; for the enjoyment of life, the wants of nature require, and the exercise of his liberty enables him to provide, from the world around him, food for his subsistence. In the pursuit of happiness, his first impulse is to the society of domestic life; by the exercise of liberty, this society is formed by mutual consent, and thus the foundation is laid of families, which, in process of time, swell into tribes, and tribes multiply into nations. The pursuit of happiness then, calls for the institution of governments, to regulate and adjust the collisions of interest and of passions, incident to the existence of civil society to secure as far as the infirmities of human nature will admit, the rights of every one, by the organized and co-operating energy of all, and to harmonize the discordant elements of the social compact.

8 Now the position to which I would invite your earnest and anxious consideration, is this: That the form of government, founded upon the principle of the natural equality of mankind, and of which the unalienable rights of individual man, are the cornerstone, is the form of government best adapted to the pursuit of happiness, as well of every individual, as of the community. It is the only actual or imaginable human government, in which self-love and social, are the same; and I think I am fully warranted in adding, that in proportion as the existing governments of the earth, approximate to, or recede from, that standard, in the same proportion, is the pursuit of happiness, of the community and of every individual belonging to it, promoted or impeded, accomplished or demolished. It is the true republic of Montesquieu the government, of which virtue is the seminal principle, and that virtue consisting of the love implanted in every bosom of the community of which it is a member.[2]

9 Of such a government, intense patriotism must be the vital spark; animated by the immortal spirit of christian benevolence, which enjoins self-love as the standard of brotherly affection, and proclaims all mankind as a brotherhood of one kindred blood. The whole soul of every citizen of such a republic, must be devoted to improve the condition of his country

2 The French philosopher Montesquieu in his seminal book, *The Spirit of the Laws*, writes that all regime types are motivated by certain organizing principles. Montesquieu argues that the rarest, hardest to maintain, and best regime is one motivated by virtue. John Quincy Adams here is claiming that the United States is one such government.

and of mankind; while liberty allows and stimulates him to the constant exercise of all the faculties of body and of mind, with which he has been endowed by his Creator, to elevate, adorn and beautify the land of his nativity, or of his choice.

Education multiplies and sharpens all these faculties. Liberty inspires 10
his head with thought, and nerves his arm for action, while patriotism supplies a perpetual incentive to exertion. Man issues from the hand of his Maker, a frail and imperfect being. His life begins in helpless infancy, and closes in the clod of the valley. Evils, physical, moral, intellectual, beset his path from the cradle to the grave, and warn him that his condition here on earth, is a state of probation, to fit him for a fairer and a better world, toward which he is wending his toilsome way; and in his progress to which, every step of improvement in his present condition, approximates him to that boundary beyond which sorrow and grief are unknown, and where the pure in spirit will find that perfection, which must be denied to them on earth.

In the pursuit of happiness, liberty is indispensable to the exercise of 11
his faculties. Were his hands given him to be manacled or tied? Were his feet given him to be fettered or cramped into impotence? How absurd do these questions appear to you; and yet, read the history of your race, and see how they have been manacled, and fettered and cramped, till their limbs have been disabled, by torture, to the purposes for which they were given to them by their Maker.

Man is a curious and inquisitive being, and the exercise of his reason, 12
the immortal part of his nature, consists of inquiries into the relations between the effects which fall within the sphere of his observation, and their causes, which are unseen. The earth beneath his feet, and the vault of heaven over his head, are the first objects, in physical nature, which force themselves upon his observation, and invite him to contemplation. The earth and the sky, elements so different in their nature, yet indissolubly united by the mysterious mandate of Almighty power, indicate to his perception, and foreshow to his reason, the condition of his own existence, compounded of body and soul, of matter and of mind. The earth ministers to each and all of his senses, the knowledge of its physical properties. He sees, hears, feels, inhales and tastes of earth and its productions, adapted to his subsistence, and to the necessities of his life on earth. The sky is accessible only to his sight, and although peopled with splendors, dazzling in

brightness and infinite in numbers, still presents to his bewildered imagination only the lights of the firmament, like a halo of glory surrounding the universe, but glowing at distances too remote to come within the reach of any other of his senses. He soon discovers, that distant as the great luminary of heaven may be from the earth, yet the earth could not exist without his generative beams; and that the heavens declare the glory of God, and the firmament sheweth forth his handy work. He turns to the heavens his eyes, and inquires what are those innumerable spangles glowing on the brow of night, and extending into the regions of infinite space, till the visual orbs of man, can no longer follow or discern them. Still he looks and searches for causes, as new celestial phenomena daily and nightly disclose themselves to his view, till the observation of the stars ripens into an art, and the germ of astronomical science has taken root in his memory. Among the earliest of his wants for the conduct of his life, are standards for the divisions of time. In the revolutions of the earth round her axis, he finds the divisions of day and night. In her revolution in her orbit round the sun, he finds the succession of years, and in the phases of the moon around herself, the measure of the month.

13 So peculiarly adapted to the nature of man, is the study of the heavens, that of all animated nature, his bodily frame is constructed as if the observation of the stars was the special purpose of his creation. This peculiar adaptation of the mechanism of the human body, has not escaped the notice of the most ingenious of the Roman poets, who, in his fabulous account of the creation, by, he knows not what God, in concluding with the production of man, says, that while other animals were formed to look downwards to the earth, he gave to man a heavenward looking face, to gaze at the sky, and commanded him to raise his head, and turn his eyes towards the stars:

Pronaque, dum spectant animalia cetera tcrram;
Os homini sublime dedit, ccelumque tueri
Juseit et erectos ad sidera tollere vultus.[3]

---

3 A quotation from Ovid's *Metamorphosis*, it roughly translates to: "Prone, while the other animals are looking at me; He gave a mouth to man on high, and to protect heaven; And raised his gaze to the stars."

Nor was it curiosity alone, which prompted the mind of the primitive man, to search the secrets of the skies. Nature unfolds to him in the structure of the firmament, scenes of unparalleled magnificence, wonder, and astonishment. In leaving to man the task of ascertaining the causes of the phenomena which he is intensely and incessantly occupied in observing, she seems devoted to the purpose of baffling his anxious inquiries, and sporting with his honest exertions. There are numerous optical illusions in the apparent movement of the heavenly bodies, and the report of the orb of vision, is never consistent with itself; never consists of the truth. The imagination becomes heated, and shadows the forms of things unknown. Superstition takes possession of the soul and the universe swarms with spectral shadows, ministering mischief and agonizing the bosom with ideal wretchedness. The first inquiry which presses itself upon the observation, is to ascertain how far the movement of the stars bears on the condition of his own existence. He sees the constant influence, beneficent or pernicious of the sun, upon the earth and all her inhabitants. He sees that the sun-beam is the source of all animal and vegetable life, and that the same sun-beam withers the plant at its root, curdles the blood in the pestilence, and speeds the bolt of death in the lightning's fork. This indissoluble connection between earth and heaven, is palpable and unquestionable. But the same firmament, in one small portion of which, the sun and his tributary planets revolve, swarms with smaller lights, besides the moon, to his untutored eye of dimensions, equal to those of the sun himself. He has not yet learnt, that relative distances cannot be measured by the apparent size of the object surveyed; but in the progress of his studies, he will discover a method of measuring heights and distances, which will refute the testimony of his naked vision, and rectify the error of his eye. He cannot fail speedily to perceive, that of the nightly visitants over his head, there are two distinct classes of stars, all apparently rising from the horizon, moving in sublime grandeur and harmony from east to west, and returning from day to day to the horizon again. So deep is this deception of the human eye, that although to the searching ken of science, the error is demonstrated, beyond the shadow of a doubt, and the fact placed beyond all controversy, that the apparent rolling of the firmament from east to west, is only the rolling of the earth round her axis from west to east, yet the stubbornness of man's belief in the testimony of his senses, never acknowledges their mistake; and all mankind, the simple and the learned; the most sublimated astronomer, 14 and the idlest school-boy, throughout their lives, continue to speak of the rising and setting of the sun, moon and stars, as if these Avere the real movements of the celestial orbs, and as if the earth, on whose surface we live, was stationed in eternal repose. Ages and ages pass away, before even the discovery of this error is made, but, in the meantime, man is continually gazing at the lamps of heaven, and in the lapse of centuries, successively detects many of their real movements, the laws by which they are regulated, their dimensions, their distances from the earth and from one another their specific gravities, and all, but the purposes of their creation. It is soon perceived, that the sun, the moon, and one of the two classes of the stars, though appearing from day to day to change their places in the celestial hemisphere, within which they are suspended, that yet, that the range of their excursive motion is confined within one narrow belt of the surrounding orb, and in the successive vicinity of one and the same portion of the clusters of stars of the second class fixed within that limited circle, while the other class of stars are apparently immoveable in the firmament, and although, moving with inconceivable velocity, yet in regions of space so remote, that the distances between them, cannot be made sensible to the human eye, so that they seem always fixed in one and the same spot of the blue expanse. They acquire thus the denomination of fixed stars. The annual revolution of the earth in her orbit round the sun, brings that luminary successively in contact, or as it is usually called, in conjunction with a succession of the same groups of stars, and while in this conjunction with them, he extinguishes, in a flood of his own splendor, all those seemingly lesser lights.

15 At an age, in the history of the earth, so remote, that the memory of it has vanished from the records of antiquity, the zone of the heavens, through the range of which the sun and planets appear to pass, has been divided into twelve clusters of equal dimensions, each passing in the compass of two hours, before the eyes of the beholder. With the aid of fancy, these constellations have been fashioned into the shape of animals, or men, and the imaginary circle has been denominated the zodiac. The superstition inspired in the early ages, into the soul of man, by the wonders unfolded to his vision, flies to the resort of fabulous invention, and a spiritual world of numberless gods is formed, which connects a tale of human action and suffering, with every constellation in the skies. From the influence of the sun upon the fortunes of the earth, and of her inhabitants, the conception

follows, that the stars, which revolve with him, must possess a proportion of the same influence; nor is the conjecture unnatural, that this influence of the sun, must be portentous, increased and various, modified when mingled with that of all the other stars, whose radiance, when in conjunction with him, is all absorbed in his own. A system of romance, is woven by superstition, into the annual revolution of the globe, and the labors of Hercules become the personification of the sun through the zodiac. The same process divides the year into twelve months, which were supposed to be of thirty days each, and thus, for many ages, the year was accounted to consist of 360 days. But the revolution of the moon round the earth, which constitutes the lunar months, is performed in twenty nine days, and from eight to sixteen hours. Twelve lunations are thus performed in 354 days. It required no very protracted experience, to ascertain, the want of five additional days, to the 360, which had been assumed as an approximation to the exact amount of one change of the four seasons. It became an object of intense interest, to discover a common measure, by which the respective periods of the sun and moon might be so combined, as to bring them to precisely the same relative position towards each other, and it was found to be of 223 lunations. But among the stars, which, in the course of each revolving year, the sun obliterates for a season, and then restores to a splendor next in glory to his own, is Sirius, or the dog star. He was worshipped as a God, by the Egyptian shepherds, and they watched his heliacal rising, after several weeks of concealment from his rays. From that day, they dated the commencement of their year. A uniform experience of centuries, disclosed to them, that, although the star regularly rises at the expiration of 365 days from his last previous emerging from the sun-beam, yet that one day more will be required for his re-appearance, at the end of every fourth year. Six hours then, was to be added, to complete the solar year, and the calendar was reformed accordingly. But this great reformation, is comparatively of modern date, having in the Roman history been first accomplished by Julius Caesar. At the end of twelve centuries, from the time when the Jewish passover, transformed into the Christian festival of Easter, by the decree of the council of Nice, in the year 325 from the birth of Christ, the precise duration of the solar year was more accurately fixed, by subtracting eleven minutes and as many seconds from the over allowance of six hours to the 365 days composing it. The Gregorian Calendar was then framed to a measurement of the solar year, consisting of 365 days, 5 hours, 48 minutes and 49 seconds, which is so near the real average time of the earth in its orbit round the sun, that there cannot be a loss of one day in less than 4000 years.[4]

16 The origin of the science of Astronomy, is lost in the darkness of antiquity. It has been ascribed to an antediluvian people, inhabiting the region of Mauritania, and of whom Atlas, the inventor of the sphere, was the king. When the race of Adam, in the progress of their degeneracy and corruptions, lost all memory of the true and only God, the Creator of the worlds, they fell into foul idolatry, surrendered themselves to all the delusions of a fiery and flighty imagination, and created numberless gods, among whom, every star had a ruling spirit. They also fancied that gifted mortals of the human family, were changed into gods, and placed among the stars. Astronomy thus became associated with false religion; and judicial Astrology, born of wild superstition, usurped the place of the genuine and legitimate science. The sun and moon were worshiped as chief, among the gods, and the fabulous invention of Greece, traced their origin to the twins of Latona, born on the Island of Delos, children of Jupiter, the father of gods and men, and sovereign of Olympus. With these attributes of power, the divinities stationed in the stars, were invested with absolute control over the fortunes and fates of every individual of the human race, and these fortunes and fates, were believed to be foreshadowed and predestined by the peculiar conjunction of certain stars, at the moment of the infant's birth. These visions of romance, were expanded and multiplied into a great, complicated system, blending together the fabrications of perverted history, the imaginations of judicial Astrology and the devoted studies of physical Astronomy. It is easy to conceive, how this amalgamation of truth and falsehood, of the most absurd forgeries of a boundless imagination, with the profound investigation of the real secrets of nature, must have obstructed the progress of the real science. From the moment that the tillage of the earth became the occupation of man, for the subsistence and multiplication of the species, it became of transcendent importance to ascertain the precise duration of the solar year, as the measure of time; and the exercise of religious worship, all adapted to the successive seasons of the year, furnished

4 The Gregorian Callender was instituted by Pope Gregory XIII as a replacement for the Julian Calendar in 1582. Though largely very similar, the Gregorian Calendar spaces leap years differently and, in so doing, more accurately approximates the earth's revolution around the sun.

from time to time the approaches to a perfect accuracy of computation. From the lunar twelve months of three hundred and fifty-four days, to the twelve equal months of thirty days each, making three hundred and sixty, and thence to three hundred and sixty-five, the approximation was effected by the revolution of the seasons themselves. The commencement of the year was fixed at the conjunction of the full moon with the vernal equinox, and then it was, that the labors of the field commenced. The Sabbath, one day in seven, was enjoined as a holiday for religious worship and for repose and refreshment, from continual toil, and the subsequent festivals throughout the year, were adapted to the day of every new moon, and to the ingathering of the harvest at the end of the year. At the Exodus of the children of Israel from Egypt, the Passover was instituted precisely at this commencement of the year, the combined full moon and vernal equinox. These institutions were, in all probability, a portion of that learning of the Egyptians, in which Moses had been initiated, and laid the foundation of the Jewish Passover, still maintained at this day in the modified form of the Christian commemoration of the day of the resurrection of their Lord and Master from the dead. All the other religious solemnities of the year, were adapted to this, and they soon brought the demonstration, that three hundred and sixty-five days were required, to complete the revolution of the year. The additional quarter of a day, was discovered by a religious festival, not of the Hebrews, but of the Egyptians, as I have already said, by the annual heliacal rising of the dog-star. And the final retrenchment of eleven minutes and eleven seconds, from the annual six hours, was again discovered in the fact, that by the celebration of the festival of Easter, for twelve hundred years, the Julian calendar had encroached on the space of real time, the amount of ten days.

To the art of Navigation, the observation of the stars is no less tributary. 17
But navigation itself is an art which can scarcely be said to have been known to the ancients. Whatever of adventure upon the ocean was undertaken by them, could extend to but very short distances from the sight of land. The straits of Gibralter, by the name of the pillars of Hercules, and the Shetland Islands, by the name of the Ultima Thule, were deemed the extremities of the earth; and less than half a century before the daring voyage of Columbus, Vasco de Gama had opened the way to India, only by doubling the Cape of Storms. The path of navigation was indeed precariously pointed out by the stars, but a beclouded sky left the mariner without

a pilot or a guide, other than the land within his sight. The polarity of the magnet, with all its yet unexplained, perhaps not inexplicable wonders, was yet a secret in the bosom of the Creator, nor has it yet been more than half revealed. To what favored mortal, the whisper of Omnipotence to man was indulged, that the suspended needle would turn in sympathy to the pole, the memory of heedless or ungrateful man, has not recorded; but notwithstanding the pretension that China, locked up in a dungeon as she has been for numberless ages, has been all the time possessed of this secret, without ever profiting by it, not withstanding that in the Odyssey of Homer, a passage of ambiguous import seems to indicate, that the man of many woes, the visitant of many cities, the crafty chieftain from Ithaca to the ten years siege of Troy, had a ministering spirit to conduct him in safety over, and through the rock bound seas. The voice of authentic history has pronounced, that the Mariner's compass was invented at Amain, in Italy, on the shores of the Mediterranean, in the twelfth century of the Christian Era.

18 In less than three centuries from that day, Christopher Columbus, of Genoa, sailed from the port of Palos in Spain, and spreading his sails to the breeze or the gale, plunged, in search of another passageway to India, into the Cimmerian darkness, of unknown oceans, with the polar needle for his only guide. He found not what he sought, the shores of Hindustan[5] by a western track: but he found what he had not imagined, two intervening continents to block up his way, little inferior in extent to the whole eastern hemisphere. Upon this discovery of the polarity of the magnetic needle, it may be remarked, as upon multitudes of other occasions in the history of human sciences, what hidden links of sympathy bind them all together. Astronomy is the study of the movements of the stars, which appear suspended in the skies at immeasurable distances from the observer. To the skies, the God of nature first commands him to turn his eyes. From the daily revolution of the Earth round her axis, the monthly revolution of the moon round the earth, and the yearly revolution of the earth and moon round the sun, a combined standard measure of time is found, uniting in harmony, the three great and indispensable divisions of days, months, and years. It is thus from the skies, that the inhabitant of the earth is provided with a measure of time, without which, the mind of man would be unconscious of its own succession of ideas, and of course unable to trace the

5 An archaic word for India.

connection between effects and their causes, and incapable of the exercise of reason. Thus it is, that

> From harmony, from heavenly harmony, This universal frame began –[6]

and thus it is, that the succession of thought, and the music of the spheres, is the chorus of Angels conveying to man the inspiration of the Almighty, which giveth him understanding.

The declination of the sun from the winter to the summer solstice 19
northward, and from the summer to the winter solstice southward of the equator, was among the earliest of Astronomical observations: It cannot escape the notice of any human eye accustomed to witness, from day to day, throughout the year, the rising and the setting sun. Its cause was reserved for the discovery of the Grecian philosopher, Anaximander, the pupil of Thales, the first of the Greeks, who devoted his talents and his life, to the investigation of the mechanism of the Universe.[7] The cause of this phenomenon is the obliquity of the ecliptic, or the angle of inclination of the plane in which the earth rolls round in her orbit, to the plane of the equator, or imaginary circle, which divides the globe into two hemispheres. From the same cause, the rising and setting of the sun, moon, and stars from day to day, is not in a perpendicular, but in a slanting direction. The arch in the firmament, daily described by the fixed stars, is, with the exception of the almost imperceptible precession of the equinoxes, always the same on any given spot of the earth but that of the sun, moon and planets, varies in right ascension from day to day; though all except the four new discovered planets, within the range of the Zodiac. In the daily arch described by the sun, his movement is, precisely half the time he is above the horizon, ascending, and half the time descending; and at the precise point of time when he ceases to ascend, and begins to culminate, the eye of the observer looking southward, meets an imaginary perpendicular line, crossing the zenith over his head, passing through the northern pole, and returning to its origin at the south. This is the meridian, and it is by the passage of the sun over this

6 This is a quotation from the English poet John Dryden's "A Song for St. Cecilia's Day."

7 Anaximander was an Ancient Greek philosopher who lived most of his life in the sixth century BC. One of the founders of ancient Greek science, he was a pioneer in geometry and astronomy. Adams' credits him with the invention of the sundial, which is a dubious historical claim.

line, that the solar day is divided into two equal parts. The passage of the heavenly bodies over this line, is thus ascertained to a second of time, and the observation of that moment, continues to this day, to be one of the most important operations of the science. Its first result was to furnish the most simple, and most perfect instrument, for the subdivision of the day into hours, minutes and seconds; the sundial invented by Anaxamander. It is but to place a spindle in the center of several concentric circles, so that the shadow of the spindle shall be formed by the rays of the sun. At whatever point of the circle, the point of the spindle terminates on the western side of the meridian line, in the morning, the interval between that point and the meridian will be precisely equal to a similar point eastward of the meridian, when the shadow of the spindle, lengthened by the descending sun, reaches the corresponding point of the same circle in the afternoon. The lapse of time for the shadow of the spindle to pass from the point west, to the meridian, and from the meridian, and the point east of the same circle, will be precisely the same. The morning measure, gives an unerring standard for the extension of the other; and the observer has a sliding scale, with which he can subdivide the solar day into as many equal parts, as his convenience, or his pleasure may require.

20 This is the principle of the Sun Dial, invented by Anaximander, and thus was obtained a perfect measure of the succession of time, from the hundredth part of a second to numbers of centuries, lost in the boundless regions of infinitude.

21 The fixation of the equinoctial and solstitial points follows close upon that of the meridian line, and they mark the bounds of the zodiac and these lead to the disclosure of the distinction between the planets, which are appendages of our solar system, and the fixed stars: themselves central suns to other systems, swarming throughout the regions of space. The planets are known by their continual apparent changes of place, on the firmament, by their alternate declination, north and south of the equator and by their varying right ascension, always observable with the naked eye. These few wanderers, amidst the numberless multitudes of apparent fixtures to the vault of heaven, were recognized in very early ages. The planets Mercury, Venus, Mars, Jupiter and Saturn, were successively discovered, and down to within our own age, were supposed, universally to be the only planets belonging to our system. Within the last century, however, the glazier and the musician have doubled the number of planets. In 1780, a musician, a

native of Germany settled in England, by long continued observation, accidentally perceived a star of the 7th magnitude, invisible to the naked eye, which had changed its place in the interval between two successive observations. The star had been marked in the catalog of Flamstead as a fixture, and since that day had performed little more than one revolution of its orbit; nor has it yet, since its discovery as a planet, completed one such revolution. The imaginary lines of the equinoxes, the solstices and the meridian were followed by two others, denominated the colures, and the armillary sphere was completed. The remarkable constellations of the zodiac, were divided into twelve signs, through each of which, the sun appears to pass in twenty-four hours. Each of these signs was historically connected with the fabulous mythology of Greece and Rome, and each star was the personification, or the abode of someone of the divinities of the heathen.

But, besides the daily occurring phenomena of the movements of the 22
sun, moon, planets and fixed stars, at all times, with a clear sky exposed to the eye, and stimulating to reflection, there are occasional phenomena happening, at distant, and unequal distances of time, striking to the eye, and terrific to the imagination. The first impression of the daily phenomena, having been that the stars themselves were animated, immortal beings, invested within definite power over the lives and fortunes of men, the incessant repetition of the same appearances, familiarized the minds of men to them, till they ceased to excite in any bosom, the sensation of hope or of fear. But it was not so with the unfrequent and unforeseen appearance of eclipses, and of comets, which never exhibited their forms in the sky, without exciting panic, terrors and agonizing distress. The eclipses of the sun and moon, usually being visible two or three times in the course of every year, lose their alarming character in proportion as their appearances multiply, and the enquiries into their causes, are multiplied and pursued by minds of various intellectual energies. The eclipses of the sun are occasioned by the passage of the moon between him and the earth, the opaque body of the moon, intercepting the rays of the sun in their passage to the earth, and the eye of the beholder resting upon the dark body of the moon. The eclipses of the moon are caused by the passage of the earth between her and the sun. The eye rests on the body of the moon, covered and darkened by the shadow of the earth, falling upon the moon in a tapering cone from the two sides of the globe, and alighting upon her disk. In both cases, the eye rests upon the body of the moon, in the solar eclipse, totally black, by

the total privation of the sun's effulgence in the lunar eclipse overshadowed by the shade of the earth herself, extended like the frustum of a cone, sometimes over the whole of the moon's disk. In a total eclipse of the sun the moon covers his whole disk, and at his place is seen nothing, but a black spot, covering his whole disk, and looking like a blot on the fair face of heaven. The eclipse of the moon always happens at the full, and with her illuminated side turns towards the earth. The light of the sun is not extinguished, but the shadow falls on her luminous disk with a dark smoky color, seldom covering her whole disk. A very small portion of the eclipses, whether of the sun or of the moon are total, and the appearances of partial eclipses are infinitely varied. Terror and consternation spread universally, at these sports of nature with the passions of man, while their causes remain unrevealed. But when once disclosed they are found to be among the simplest and most harmless operations of nature. The interposition of an opaque body, between the light of a lamp, and any object upon which it sheds its beams, produces all the apparitions visible in these planetary conjunctions and oppositions, and reveals the whole theory of solar and lunar eclipses. By continual persevering observation of the skies, the discovery cannot fail to be made, and when the measure of time, comes once to be made, and the periodical revolutions of the sun moon and planets, combined together, are so perfectly ascertained it is one of the easiest tasks of the Astronomer, to predict within a minute of time, when any given eclipse of the sun or moon will take place, for thousands of years to come: and there are memorable instances in history, of the use made by a nation possessed of this secret, to subdue their enemies uninstructed of the same knowledge. That it was known to the ancient Chaldeans, is known by the calculations of eclipses found by Callisthenes at Babylon, and transmitted to Alexander, embracing a period backward in the lapse of time, of more than two thousand years. The annexation and adherence of comets to our solar system, is a secret among the more recondite mysteries of nature; and signalized by exhibitions to the vision of man, still more terrific and astounding than those of the eclipses. The intervals between the apparitions of those fiery visitors from infinite space, are longer and more frequent than of eclipses. The phenomena attending the appearance of comets, are of occurrence so rare, their movements are so irregular, and the fiery trail that they draw behind them is so terrific, that their existence, and the laws by which they are governed as part of our system, are far less accessible to the observation of the human eye, than the revolutions of the planets. Two centuries have not yet elapsed since the discovery made by Dr. Halley; that the comets have, like the planets, stated periods of revolution in their elliptical orbits round the sun. But their numbers, and the extent of their range over infinite space in the firmament, are not yet known, nor likely to be so, for centuries to come. The continual variations from day to day, of the declinations and right ascension of the planets, indicating movements precisely similar to those of the sun and moon, soon lead to the conclusion that they form a part of one system. The planets Mercury, Ve nus, Mars, Jupiter and Saturn, form together a combination of co- temporaneous movements, which it requires ages of continuous observation to disentangle. The earth herself with her attendant satellite, the moon, is one of the planets; though being the abode of the observer, and her surface the station from which he observed, he has not the same elements for calculation of her movements as of the rest. It is soon found that the orbits of Mercury and Venus, are included within that of the earth, and those of Mars, Jupiter and Saturn, at proportionate lengthened distances from the sun, as the distance of each planet increases its orbit, enlarges and encloses within itself the orbits of all the planets nearer to the sun than itself. Thus, as the orbit of the earth includes within itself those of Venus and Mercury, and is included within those of Mars, Jupiter and Saturn, the simultaneous observation of all these movements, runs into a scrall inexplicable to all but the most intense application and perseverance of the human intellect. The revolution of the planet Mercury round the sun, is performed in the space of three months that of the earth in one year that of Jupiter in twelve, and that of Saturn in thirty years. All these discoveries were made by the Astronomers of antiquity. It was reserved for the vision of an observer of the eighteenth century, to discover the planet now called Uranus, the revolution of which, in its orbit is performed in 80 years. Since which, four other planets have been discovered within the region, between Mars and Jupiter. Of these last four planets, there is this remarkable peculiarity, that their orbits, much interlocked with each other, extend beyond the belt of the zodiac. The daily variation of the declination and right ascension of the sun and moon, are so conspicuous to the eye of every beholder, that they cannot escape notice for any length of time. The star planets exhibit varieties of movement of the same character, less exposed to the naked vision; but being objects of so much smaller apparent size, are not so easily or so soon detected ; bat are ultimately recognized as parts of the same organized, complicated machine. The process of Astronomical discovery, is uniform in its operation. The object is first perceived as it presents itself to the eye. When that is sufficiently fixed, the reasoning faculty commences the search for causes, and then the inventive powers are put in requisition, for the application to useful purposes, of the discoveries that have been made. In observing the revolutions of the planets in their orbits, the optical delusions are multiplied, the movements themselves are complicated, consisting of the movement of the planet itself, combined with the simultaneous movement of the earth, and the alternate conjunction and opposition of the sun; and they give to the movement of the planet, the deceptive appearance of irregular motion; sometimes direct, at others retrograde now. slackening, and now accelerated, and occasionally stationary but patient and persevering observation, discloses all the thread of the texture,

> "Untwisting all the ties, that bind
> The hidden soul of harmony."[8]

23 Whatever of Astronomical science may have been acquired by the earliest Asiatic and African monarchies, which succeeded the confusion of Babel, the first schools of philosophy in Greece, are known to have originated about six hundred and fifty years before the Christian sera. Thales of Miletus, is the first of the Grecian sages known to posterity, as having been versed in the science of Astronomy, and as having contributed to its progress. He was cotemporary with the prophet Jeremiah, and with king Ahaz, whose sun dial was the subject of a miracle, which proves beyond all question, that the use of the dial was familiarly known, and had been so for ages, in the kingdom of Judah. The Argonautic expedition is the first event in Grecian history, showing the existence of a confederated government, carrying with it an art of navigation, and a science of Astronomy. Thales was the first of the wise men of Greece, and is, also, the first of Grecian Astronomers. He acquired in Egypt, all the astronomical knowledge that he possessed; and is said to have taught the Egyptian priests to measure the height of the pyramids, by the length of their shadows. He founded

8 A line borrowed from Adams' favorite poet, John Milton, in his work "L'Allegro."

the Ionian school of philosophy.[9] He taught that the stars are of the same substance with the Earth, but kin dled into a flame. That the light of the moon is but borrowed from the sun. That she causes the eclipses of the sun, by inter posing between the sun and the moon, and that the moon is eclips ed by the shadow of the earth. He taught that the earth was a globe, and divided into five circles, the arctic and antarctic, the two tropics and the equator. The obliquity of the ecliptic, and the perpendicular of the meridian, were also familiar to his school. The circles of the sphere are a mechanical invention, to describe the regions of the earth, and corresponding regions of the heavens : the forms of the constellations, and the distribution of the fixed stars. Yet two hundred and fifty years after his death, the first of the Greek historians, Herodotus, in speaking of a solar eclipse, says, that the sun abandoned his place in the' skies, and left it to night. Thales is said to have been the first man who foretold a solar eclipse. It is said, also, that he measured the diameter of the sun.

His successor in the Ionian school, Anaximander, was the inventor of 24
geographical maps. And he was the first, who held that the sun, was a ball of fire, with the earth revolving round it. He believed, also, in the plurality of worlds; and held, also, that the moon receives her light from reflection, from the sun, but has, besides, a feebler light of her own. Anaximander was succeed ed by Anaximenes, of the same city, and said to have been, the inventor of the sun-dial. But, this is not possible, for it has been remarked, that the sun-dial was familiarly known in the days of Ahaz, who lived 200 years before Anaximenes. There is no doubt, that the dial was a Chaldean invention, and it is highly probable, that the pyramids, were among other uses, intended for dials, on a larger scale.

Anaxagoras of Clazomene,[10] was the disciple and successor of Anax- 25
imenes. Like all the Grecian philosophers, in speculating upon the visible objects of the Creation, in eager pursuit of the causes of the natural phenomena exposed to the senses, whenever the fact did not appear sufficient for its own explanation, they resorted to conjecture, and they formed theories so wild, and extravagant, that we now wonder how they could ever have entered into the heads of rational men. Anaxagoras was so much

9 A pre-Socratic school of philosophy that is credited with many advances in early science and mathematics.

10 A pre-Socratic philosopher who, among many other accomplishments, deduced the causes of eclipses.

absorbed in the contemplation of the heavens, that he neglected his worldly concerns; that, upon being asked, whether he had no time for his country, he pointed to the sky, and exclaimed, there is my country. Yet, Anaxagoras, from the single fact, of the falling of a stone from the sky, a phenomenon of repeated, and well authenticated occurrence, both in the old and in the new world, imagined that the whole firmament was one mass of stone. That the stars, were small parcels of the substance of the earth, evaporated from the agency of fire, and suspended, as inflamed globes, in the atmosphere. He maintained, also, that the sun was a blazing torch, larger than the Peloponessus, and that the moon was larger than the earth.

26 For these, and other profound and ingenious speculations, upon the nature of matter, and of mind, Anaxagoras was, as usual, persecuted. He was a Unitarian, and declared his opinion, that there was but one God.[11] He taught the true causes of eclipses, by the interposition of the moon between the earth and the sun, and of the interposition of the earth between the sun and the moon. He was accused of impiety to the Gods, for believing that there was but one God, and for affirming, what is now universally known to be true, that eclipse is nothing more than the interposition of an opaque body, between a luminary and the object on which it shines. He was accused of impiety to the Gods tried convicted, and condemned to death: which sentence, at the suggestion of Pericles, was commuted for banishment.

27 The opinions of Anaxagoras, upon the materiality, size, distance, and relative magnitude of the sun, moon, and stars, illustrate the progress of the science of Astronomy, in enlarging the compass of the human mind, as well as the immensity of the material universe. That the mind of Anaxagoras was of the highest order of human intellect, is evident from the nature of the subjects on which it habitually, perseveringly and passionately dwelt. The mind, capable of rising, by its native energies, to the conception of one, and only one Supreme Ruler of the universe capable of ascending to the idea of its own ultimate destination in the skies, was of no ordinary stamp and yet, how infinitely small, was the range of its contemplations, when we find it estimating the mass of matter in the sun, as comparable, in volume, to that

11 Adams' use of the term "unitarian" here is slightly misleading. Usually used to refer to someone in the Christian tradition who denies the trinity, Adams seems to be using the term to mean monotheism – the belief in one single God rather than many. In the age of ancient Greece, this would have been considered a serious religious offense.

of the Peloponnese; the moon larger than the earth, and the stars as parcels of this terrestrial globe itself! When we see the first Herschel, bring within the field of one glance of his telescope, 36,000 solar systems in a nebula, into what nothing, sink the estimates of Anaxagoras.

The Ionian school, was transferred by Anaxagoras and Archelaus, from 28
Miletus to Athens, while, about the same time, another school of philosophy, was founded by Pythagoras. This is one of the most remarkable personages of all antiquity, and his principal residence having been at Crotona, his school was known by the name of the Italic.[12] His system of philosophy, like that of Thales, embraced the principles of morals, no less than the science of physical nature. He had, before attempting to introduce his institution, established a reputation for wisdom and virtue, so transcendent, that his moral instructions were issued, in the form of self-evident truths, and indisputable commands, so that, if upon any precept given by him, any question was ever made, the answer of his disciples, "*He said it*," silenced all objections. In our own times, in all the intercourse of society, there is a freedom of thought, and of speech, held so inviolable, that we find it difficult to believe that such despotic authority of intellect, should ever have been established, and submitted to, between man and man, otherwise equals. Pythagoras, was a native of the Island of Sidon, the son of a sculptor, of Samos, and bred to the profession of a common wrestler. But, in attendance upon the discourses of Pheracydes[13], on the immortality of the soul, his own spirit took wing to the future world, and he devoted his life to philosophy. Morals, Politics, Mathematics, Astronomy, Natural History, and domestic economy, all were included in his school of philosophy, for the very name of which, the world is indebted to him. He modestly disclaimed the name of sage, or wise man, which the distinguished men of learning, had assumed, before him, and called himself, only a lover of wisdom. In every department of intellectual improvement, no individual of the human race, without the bounds of divine inspiration, ever bestowed more rays of light, upon the soul of his fellow creature, man, than Pythagoras. His golden verses, are rules of life, as admirable at this day, as when first composed. His rules of justice, and mercy, and of sympathy with the human race, approach as near to Christian perfection, as ever had been attained before the advent

12 Crotona is the modern-day Crotone in southern Italy.

13 A little-known Greek philosopher who some (including Adams) believe to have been the teacher of Pythagoras.

of the Messiah. He was the discoverer of that mathematical theorem, the foundation of trigonometry, navigation; the mensuration of heights and distances I might almost say, of all mathematics a discovery not made by accident, or mere good fortune ; but, wrought out with the most elaborate mental exertions, and for which, when accomplished, he is said to have exclaimed, "I have found it: and sacrificed a hecatomb to the Gods." The immense stride in the advancement of the science of Astronomy, by this discovery between the sides of a right-angled triangle, can scarcely be conceived; but, Pythagoras is further entitled to the credit, of having given the first hint of the Copernican system, now universally admitted, that the earth revolves round the sun.

29 The next most renowned Grecian contributor, to the science of Astronomy, was Meton, the calculator, who invented the cycle of 19 years, which bears his name, and is familiar to all our almanacs, under the name of golden number.[14] It rests upon the assumption, that, 19 solar years, are in time, precisely equal to 235 lunar months, which is correct within a space of two hours. Meton presented the tables, and an explanation of his cycle, at the Olympic games, of Greece, 432 years before Christ; it was immediately accepted, and the first cycle commenced with that year. It has continued, to the present time, and the golden number of the present year, is l.

30 The age of Socrates, and Plato, followed close upon that of Meton, and, it is generally believed, that Socrates, by confining his philosophical investigations to mind, and morals, rather discouraged, than promoted, the application of the faculties of the soul, to the phenomena of physical nature. A similar prejudice has prevailed among many of the eminent teachers of mankind, from that time to the present, whether, because the study of physical nature, combined with that of the mathematics (and, without this combination, nothing useful to mankind can ever be accomplished by the study,) necessarily requires more painful and toilsome exercise of the intellectual faculties, than speculations upon morals, religion, politics, and the sports of imagination; or, whether, in these studies, there is something more congenial to the nature of a being, compounded of perishable and immortal elements, the philosophers of associated man, have found more favor with their pupils, than the searchers into causes, necessarily leading up to the first cause, impenetrable to human search. The vulgar fable of the

14 Meton was an ancient Greek philosopher who discovered that the lunar cycles repeat almost exactly every nineteen years.

Astronomer, who, in gazing upon the stars, stumbles into a ditch, though, probably, first devised only to deride the devotion of weak and superstitious minds, to the absurd and baseless visions of Astrology, has an unfortunate tendency, to deter the inclinations of the young, from the sublimest and the most useful of all contemplations, to the meditative and energetic mind, the structure of that universe, of which itself is an imperishable, though an infinitely diminutive atom. The poet, who sang, the proper study of mankind, is man, narrowed down the faculties of the human soul to a nut-shell.[15] Man, is, no doubt, the proper study of mankind, but, so is nature. So is that world, in which he is placed, in probation, with rights to enjoy, and duties to fulfill. So is that Being, all-wise, all good, all powerful, his creator, and his judge. So is that firmament, over his head. So is that earth, under his feet. So is that atmosphere, which is his breath of life. So are those waters, over which he must learn to float, but in which he cannot live. So are those animal, vegetable, and mineral realms of nature, given him by the bounty of his Maker, for food and raiment, for strength, beauty, and grace. All, all, are studies for mankind, as proper, and as necessary, as man himself.

And such, no doubt, was the sentiment of Socrates, and of Plato. We 31
know, that it was in the school of Plato, that the Greeks learnt to trace the causes of the celestial phenomena; though his own conjectures of those causes, the cycle and epicycle, orb in orb, were erroneous. His friend, Eudoxus, like himself, sought for learning among the priests of Egypt. He learnt, also, from the Chaldeans, and, although he made no discoveries himself, he had the merit of separating the real, from the spurious science, and of devoting himself to the study of Astronomy, while he rejected, and spurned, the imposture of Astrology.

He was followed by Aristotle, Pytheas, and the Alexandrian school. 32
Eudemus, and Theophrastus, wrote each a history of Astronomy, but neither of those works has been preserved from the scythe of Time.[16] The poem of Aratus, on the phenomena of the heavens, more fortunate, has not only survived, but has enjoyed the glorious privilege, of two several translations, into Latin verse; by two of the most illustrious names of Republican

15 In his poem, "Essay on Man," Alexander Pope famously declared "The proper study of mankind is man."

16 Eudemus of Rhodes and Theophrastus of Lesbos were associates of Aristotle. Most of their work has been lost.

and Imperial Rome by Cicero, and by Germanian Cesar.[17] Aratus was the first, who gave a new charm to the study of Astronomy, by connecting it with the fascinating beauties, and irresistible charms of poetry. He lived in the age of that pattern of monarchs, patron of literature, science, and the liberal arts, Ptolemy Philadelphus.[18] His museum, the first great establishment founded by royal munificence, for the cultivation of mind, contributed more than any other institution, of antiquity, to the improvement of mankind, and the elevation of the human character. There it was, that Hipparchus laid the foundations of the modern sciences of Astronomy and of Geography The invention of the armillary sphere. The first catalogue of the stars. The discovery of the precession of the equinoxes; and the calculation in advance, of the eclipses of six hundred years, are in the history of Astronomy, achievements for which the men of all after ages, are indebted to Hipparchus.[19] He flourished, in the interval between 160 and 125 years before Christ, and the next great luminary of the Alexandrian school, was Ptolemy, not of the royal race of that name, but of a far brighter name, as the author of that system of Astronomy, denominated, many centuries after by its Arabian translators, the Almagest, or great work, by which it is known to this day.[20] He was born in Ptolemais, in Egypt; his observations at Alexandria, were made under the reigns of the Roman Emperors, Adrian and Antoninus Pius, from the year 125 to 139, of the Christian era; 250 years had, of course, elapsed, since the Alexandrian school had been illustrated by the labors of Hipparchus. During that interval, the reformation of the Roman Calendar, by Julius Caesar, the purest and most glorious of the titles of that heroic monster, to renown, had been established. The measurement of time, by the combined diurnal rotation of the earth upon her axis, and the annual revolution round the sun, is the only certain regulator of human history, of religious devotion and of domestic life. The first Roman year of Numa, was the lunar year of 354 days. It had been successively altered to twelve equal months, of thirty days, and to the subsequent addition of five supplementary days. It had long been discovered, that the solar year,

17 Aratus was an ancient Greek poet, most famous for a long poem on the constellations.

18 An Egyptian pharaoh who patronized the arts in the Alexandrian period.

19 Hipparchus was an ancient Greek astronomer who invented trigonometry and was the first scientist to truly understand the equinoxes.

20 He is referring here to Claudius Ptolemy, a noted Alexandrian philosopher.

consisted of a fragment of a day more than 365; and, in the approximation to the real fact, one quarter of a day, or one day in four years, had been assumed as the addition necessary to be made, to equalize the year of the Calendar with the equation of time. Many years, and not seldom, many ages, elapse, after the secrets of nature have been detected by the ingenuity, industry, and perseverance of man, before he avails himself of them for the improvement of his own condition. So it was, with the Roman Calendar, till the Julian reform. It answered its purposes for 1500 years. Centuries before the expiration of that period, it had been ascertained that the addition of six hours a year to the 365 days, was too long for the natural year. The Calendar was again reformed, by Pope Gregory, the 13th, to restore the true scriptural day, for the celebration of the resurrection of the Savior. Yet, such was the protestant prejudice, against this most salutary and useful improvement, that the learned, ingenious, and generous nation of which we were then members, resisted its establishment until beyond the middle of the last century; and the Greek church, of the immense Empire of Russia, resists its introduction even to this day; preferring to celebrate the most solemn of their religious festivals that of the resurrection of the dead, on a day notoriously different from that prescribed by the Savior himself, rather than adopt the decree issued by the supreme head of a sister church, followers of the same Lord and Master.[21]

The mind of Julius Cesar, then, enlarged, comprehensive, liberal in the 33
exercise of power, then not acquired by crime, appropriated to the benefit of the Roman world, in their measurement of time, the discoveries of the Grecian school of Alexandria; but the Romans, themselves, made no discoveries in Astronomy. Hipparchus, was the first great luminary, of the Alexandrian school. Ptolemy, was the second and last. Between them, they constructed a theory of the universe; a system of created nature; founded, indeed, upon that optical illusion, which first arrests the inquiries of man, into the mechanism of the world around him, but which was destined to vanish, in process of time, before the persevering searching of a future age. In contemplating that stupendous, apparent revolution of the whole firmament of heaven round the earth, performed day after day, under his eye, the royal psalmist of Judea, bursts forth into a shout of glory, to the Creator,

21 The Eastern Orthodox Church to this day refuses to adopt the Gregorian Callender and thus celebrates religious festivals on a different timeline than the majority of Christian sects.

and particularly describes the circuit of the sun, from his rising in the east, to his descent beneath the horizon, in the opposite quarter of the sky. But human observation, progresses to a system, by detecting the phenomena of nature, one by one. They accumulate, in a course of ages, and then range themselves into a system. Neither Hipparchus, nor Ptolemy, disciplined their souls to the hardihood of setting at defiance, the testimony of their eyes, and of assuming, that the appearance of the rotation of the firmament, was only the rotation of the earth herself round her axis; but the precession of the equinoxes, the obliquity of the ecliptic, the double system of movements, regulating the different movements of the fixed stars, and the planets, and even the parallaxes of the bodies congregated in the solar system, had been discovered by or before Hipparchus, and were now organized into a system by Ptolemy. Trusting to the optical delusion of the eye, he assumed, that the earth was at rest at the center of the universe, around which, all the heavenly bodies daily revolved but the relative positions, movements, and distances of the sun, moon, and the planets Mercury, Venus, Mars, Jupiter and Saturn had been calculated and made known by Hipparchus, and were now wrought up into a celestial mechanism, by Ptolemy. That the material substance of all these bodies, was spherical, had been as certain, by long contested and multiplied demonstrations, and the natural conclusion, that their revolutions round the orbits was also necessarily circular, was another error, that nothing less than the lapse of many centuries, and the minds of Tycho, of Kepler, and of Newton, could redeem.

34 The science of Astronomy, is the intercourse of immortal man with the universe. The mind, accustomed to contemplate with inquisitive and persevering research, the wonders of the creation, enlarges itself by the constant exercise of its powers, as steel is at once sharpened and brightened, by continual attrition. The genius of Ptolemy, was not confined to communion with the stars. Besides, that common chain, which unites, as with links of adamant, the whole circle of the sciences, and the liberal arts, there is a still more close and intimate connection of Astronomy with Geography, and with optics, and the various branches of the Mathematics, than with the rest. The pillars of the fame of Ptolemy, repose not less upon his system of Geography, than upon his Astronomy. He was the author, also, of a treatise of optics, which, although known to have been extant in the eleventh and thirteenth centuries, perished in the Gothic barbarism of the Middle Ages. It is easy to perceive, (says the profound and ill-starred Bailly)

that few men have labored so much, and upon more important objects, than Ptolemy. He embraced chronology, music, optics, and dialing, after ruling as the legislator of Astronomy and Geography. He is said to have died, at the age of 78 years. And a saying of his, has been recorded, characteristic of that conscious superiority of genius, over the conventional greatness of human institution, which belongs to the benefactors of mankind: On being invited to the table of a monarch, he declined the honor, observing, that "kings, like paintings, are made to be seen from a distance."

The glory of the Alexandrian school, finished with Ptolemy. His system 35
became the scientific creed of the world, and, as it was founded on a basis of error, its semblance of truth itself, arrested for a thousand years, the progress of the human mind, towards the real truth. Assuming, that the earth was the center of the solar system, round which all the heavenly bodies revolved in circular orbits, the movements of the planets in different directions, sometimes from east to west, at others from west to east, and then, again, stationary, became inexplicable to the theory of a simple and steady movement in a circular orbit, and required an imaginary complicated machinery of cycle and epicycle, orb in orb, supposing a separate organization of the motions for each separate planet, without connecting link, or observation of a single principle, impelling them all.

Then came the conquest of the Arabian imposter, and the burning, by 36
his ignorant and barbarian Lieutenant Omar, of that magnificent library of Alexandria. But the science scornfully rejected by the fanaticism of a new religion, resumed again her grasp upon the soul of man, by the lure of superstition. Till the age of Mahomet, the Arabian Astronomers had been of the Chaldean and Egyptian schools. The stars had been their Gods. Sirius, Aldebaran, Canopus had been the objects of their worship.[22] The doctrine preached by Mahomet and his followers, consisted of two plain clear and intelligible principles. The unity of God, and the prophetic mission of Mahomet. So irresistibly did the first of these principles, once proclaimed, seize hold of the avenues to the heart, that it carried down the second with it. There is but. one God, and Mahomet is his prophet, was the triumphant shout of victory, and at the same time the whole creed of the warrior Muslim, from Mecca to Tontarabia. The stars ceased to be Gods. The Syrian, the Egyptian, and the Greek and Roman deities all perished in the conflagration of the Alexandrian library, before the unity of God and

22 A series of prominent stars.

the prophetic mission of the Camel driver. But from their ashes sprung up a new swarm of spiritual rulers of the destinies of man. The stars were still instinct with life, with occult mysterious agency in waving the wand of fate over the lives and fortunes of the only rational tenant of this terrestrial Globe.

37 We must remember, that of the genuine and the spurious science, of the chaste matron and the painted harlot; the parentage is one and the same. They are sisters of one and the same descent, and their family features are so much alike, that it requires almost the eye of intuition to distinguish the virtue from the vice. The study of Astronomy and of Astrology both, consist of a mere comparison between the relative location in infinite space; and movements of the heavenly bodies in their aspects towards one another. The firmament consists of innumerable multitudes of these shining bodies suspended in the immensity of space, moving in silent harmony, and incomprehensible order, day after day, over the head of man, from the cradle to the grave. They are exposed to the perception of only one of his senses, the eye inaccessible to all the rest. What they are, whence they came, where they are going, and how they exist, suspended upon nothing he knows not, but is left to discover, by the combining and discriminating powers of his intellect. None of the machinery which he invents to assist him in his researches, exist in nature. They are round, as they appear to his eye; the sun and moon, with disks of considerable dimensions; the largest of the stars, scarcely bigger than the head of a pin, and the rest tapering off into graduated magnitude, to a barely discernible point, and still swarming, as the power of vision fails, but all apparently round. The earth on which he dwells, never appears to him as one of these stars of the firmament; till after ages upon ages of observation, he finds she is one of the smallest of them. A satellite of the sun, and still round; spherical, though not a perfect sphere. To study the nature of these immeasurable masses, he must divide them into parts. He constructs then, artificial globes, and divides them into circles of latitude and longitude of three hundred and sixty degrees, sub-divided into minutes and seconds. He provides them with poles, with an equator, a zodiac, and an ecliptic, a zenith, and a nadir's equinoctial and solstitial points, polar circles, tropics and colures. Of all this, there is nothing in nature, neither the globe of earth, nor the firmament of heaven; they are merely human inventions, to assist the observations of man in his searches after physical truth. But all this machinery is

equally used by the Astronomer and the Astrologer. And as they compare the relative positions of the heavenly bodies, in their complicated motions, the bodies which cross each other's paths, appear in reference to each other, in different aspects, known alike to the Astronomer and the Astrologer, as in conjunction, or in opposition, in quadrature or in trine.

The various, different, and in many respects, opposite motives which 38
have impelled mankind to the study of the stars, have had a singular effect in complicating and confounding the nomenclature of the science. Religion, idolatry, superstition, curiosity, the thirst for knowledge, the passion for penetrating into the secrets of nature, the warfare of the huntsman by night and by day, against the beasts of the forest and of the field. The meditations of the shepherd in the custody and wanderings of his flocks and herds, the influence of the revolving seasons of the year, and the successive garniture of the firmament, upon the labors of the husband man, upon the seed time and the harvest, the blooming of flowers, and the ripening of the vintage, the polar pilot of the navigator, and the mysterious magnet of the mariner all in harmonious action, stimulate the child of earth and of heaven, to interrogate the dazzling splendors of the sky, to reveal to him the laws of their own existence. He sees his own comforts, his own happiness, his own existence identified with theirs. He sees the Creator in creation, and calls upon creation to declare the glory of the Creator. When Pythagoras the philosopher of the Grecian schools, conceived that more than earthly idea of the music of the spheres, when the darling dramatist of nature, inspires the lips of his lover on the moonlight green, with the beloved of his soul to say to her

Sit Jessica - Look how the floor of heaven,
Is thick inlaid with patterns of bright gold.
There's not the smallest orb which thou beholdest,
But in his motion, like an angel sings,
Still choiring, to the young eyed cherubim.[23]

Oh! who is the one with a heart, but almost wishes to cast off this muddy vesture of decay, to be admitted to the joy of listening to the celestial harmony.

23 The quote is from William Shakespeare's *The Merchant of Venice*. Spoken by Lorenzo to his beloved Jessica as they gaze upon a starry sky.

39 As the motives in the mind of man, urging him to the study of the stars, are so powerful, and so multifarious, so are the modes of pursuing this study, equally numerous and diversified. The sun, the moon, and the two classes, the wandering and the sedentary stars, so seemingly alike to the first inspection; so utterly and increasingly unlike on close, and closer examination; the special search for discovery of each individual planet, and for the laws of their existence and movements, whether common to them all, or separate to each individual; the burning splendor of Mercury, so minute, as to be seldom visible to the naked eye, yet so dazzling bright when seen; the lunar phases of Venus, most brilliant in her quarter, and inextinguishable, even in the presence of the sun. The special privilege of these two planets to pass occasionally, though rarely, over the face of the sun in the sight of man, and at times, predicted to the fraction of a second by him; the rubicund visage, and snow bleached pole of Mars; the belts and satellites of Jupiter; the satellites and rings of Saturn; the planetary character, and satellites of Uranus, mistaken by Flamsteed for a fixed star of the sixth magnitude, and finally, the quadruple fragment of one large planet; which, to preserve the symmetry of the solar system, should have been stationed between Mars and Jupiter, all the fragments discovered in that region, but ranging in eccentric orbits, beyond the bounds of the ecliptic, in which the sun, and all the other discovered planets are confined; all these have been, and yet, are made the special subjects of keen and acute observation, of stubborn and incessant research, and of elaborate calculation. Then the world of comets, travelers, perhaps, into the regions of more than one solar system, and in their parabolic orbits, passing successively from one to another, a theme but recently, and yet imperfectly opened to exploring enquiry. To all this, has been added of late years, with the new auxiliary assistance of stupendously increased magnifying glasses, indefatigable and unceasing labors, to enumerate, and classify, and publish catalogs of the fixed stars. Of more than one of them parallaxes, have been at length ascertained, and distances of almost inexpressible numbers, have been measured and recorded; double, triple and quadruple stars, having separate movements of mutual connection with each other, have been detected, and allured to further discovery. And while the star gazers, from Observatories, multiplying in the four quarters of the globe, almost in proportion to the multiplication of the new discovered stars themselves, force upon the mind of man, the conclusion, that every new accession to his knowledge, acquired by his

unceasing and untiring efforts, are but spurs to stimulate the ever restless activity of his intellectual powers, for the acquisition of more. When, and how, and by whom the zodiac, as it is now exhibited in all our celestial maps, and all our annual almanacs, was invented, no effort of learning, has yet been able to discover. Its origin is undoubtedly fabulous, connected with the whole system of the mythology of Greece, with the twelve labors of Hercules, the expedition of the Argonauts to Colchis, for the golden fleece; the genealogy of Jupiter, Neptune and Pluto, their common parent Saturn, and the final solution of the whole system, in the allegorical impersonation of heaven and earth. Here Astronomy, and Astrology, idolatry and superstition, agriculture and navigation, all march hand in hand, turning history into romance, religion into falsehood; the cultivation of the earth, and the navigation of the seas into fraudulent imposture. By what magical incantation, the belief of this system could be imposed upon whole nations of men, imagination can scarcely conceive. An imaginary belt is cast around the portion of the heavens, within which, the solar system revolves. This belt is divided into twelve partitions, each embracing thirty degrees of the spherical circumference. Within each of these partitions, clusters of stars, as they are visible in the sky, are gathered as into one community; and over each of them, the figure of an earthly animal is stamped, covering the whole constellation, but bearing no sort of resemblance to it. The very positions, and attitudes of the animals are painted on the celestial atlas, names are given to all the brightest of the stars, and now, at least three thousand years after this uncouth fiction was first palmed upon the credulity of mankind, we find it imposed upon us still, and we cannot learn to recognize the bright stars of heaven in the path of the sun, without painting them to the mind's eye, on the horns of a reposing ram, in the eye of a raging bull, on the foreheads of a pair of twin children, and in the fantastic and incoherent imagery of animals, wild and tame, of earth, air, fire and water, jumbled together, as if to resolve the created universe, into its primitive elemental chaos. Nor is this wild, and scarcely conceivable confusion yet exhausted. When 'the worship of idols, had thus insinuated itself into communion with the study of Astronomy, the population of the zodiac was extended over the whole firmament. The chief of the gods, Jupiter, and even the inferior idols of Olympus, were invested with the prerogative, of placing favorite mortals to seats of honor in the heavens; and thus, not only Hercules and Perseus, but Adonis and Narcissus and Daphne, and Niobe and her daughters, and multitudes of others, not more meritorious, rose to be dignitaries in the skies; till not only the hair of Berenice, became a constellation, and the infamous Antinous, a star of resplendent magnitude. To crown this infatuation of besotted learning, modern Astronomers, impelled by usurping vanity or base adulation, have assumed the presumption of placing among the stars, not only the shield of Sobiesky, and the crown of the Prussian Frederic, with the scepter of Brandenburg, but have cast to the hunting dogs, the rotten heart of Charles the first. The printing press, the electrical apparatus, and the air pump, may be better entitled to this symbol of immortality, but their intrusion upon this, already overcharged canvas, only adds to its unnatural complication, and encumbers the study with supernumerary difficulties and obstructions.

40 The cultivation of Astronomy, by the Arabians of the middle ages, during the learned period of their caliphs Haroun-al-Raschid, Almanzcr and Almamon, added little or nothing to the progress of the science. They preserved it from decay by their translation of the great work of Ptolemy, and by their diligent enumeration of the stars, and their assiduity in giving them names. It is said that no nation has ever given so many names to the stars; but even that, is not without its inconveniencies to the modern student of Astronomy. Whoever is conversant with the celestial charts or globes, finds himself embarrassed with double and treble systems of notation. With Greek, Latin and Arabic names, all different, but affixed to the same stars with letters of the Greek, Roman alphabets, often added to their names, and in many cases, the same Arabic names given to several stars in different Constellations.

41 Happy, said the greatest of the Roman poets of the Augustan age, happy the man who has been able to ascertain the causes of things.[24] To trace the causes of things, is, of all the animal creation, the exclusive propensity, and faculty of man. He is the only animated being privileged to enquire into causes. Happy, then, must he be, when indulgent nature condescends to answer his enquiries. Of the antediluvian study of Astronomy, no record is left; but from the time of the dispersion of mankind, from the plain of Sennaar, the study of Astronomy, and the search for the causes of its phenomena, have been unremitting. In the obscurity of remote antiquity, all that we can discern is, that Astronomy, Astrology, and the Pantheon of Paganism rose and flourished together. With the first glimpse of Astronomy,

24 Adams here is very loosely quoting Virgil's *Georgics*.

which has come down to us; are associated all the gods of the Greeks, long settled upon their thrones in the stars. The zodiac was already peopled, with its twelve signs and constellations, and the only indication we have of the time when it was established, is the fact, that it fixed the point of the vernal equinox, at the first degree of the constellation of the ram. Thales and Pythagoras, the founders of the Ionian and Italian schools of philosophy, are the first who appear to have made the study of the stars, a subject of philosophical inquiry, to trace the causes of things; but the gods had been settled on Mount Olympus, long before the time of Homer, who lived, and whose epic poems had been composed at least five hundred years before Thales or Pythagoras were born. The zodiac itself is an imaginary bandage of twelve successive clusters of stars, marking in the heavens the annual apparent path of the sun, but the real path of the earth; but what ages of successive observations, must have passed away before those successive groups of stars could have been gathered into conventional communities, stamped with the images of certain animals, and committed to the custody of certain deities, before they could be recognized and worshiped as gods.

With every sign of the zodiac, with every one of the planets, and with 42
all the remarkable constellations of the northern hemisphere, there was connected a historical fable and traditional biography, of men, who had made themselves conspicuous for good or evil, during their lives, and who were worshiped as gods, or doomed to Tartarus for their crimes after death. The study of the stars, then, was a whimsically compounded system of religion, of real and fabulous history, and of Astronomy, of which the metamorphoses of Ovid are, perhaps, the most characteristic exponents. The first attempts to separate these most incongruous and incoherent elements of philosophical inquiry, superstition and history, were made by Thales and Pythagoras, and they appear to have been, both by different ways, on the real track in their search for the detection of causes, and the discovery of truth. But the first and greatest obstacle to the progress of that study, comes from superstition, which, at that stage of human society is identical with religion. Thales was the first of philosophers, that is, of searchers for that happiness, which the Mantuan bard avers flows from ascertaining the causes of things.

But the worship of idols, is the first great error of man, in the state of 43
nature. His unassisted mind has not energy to conceive the foundation of all truth, that there is one, and only one God, the Creator, and the ruler

of the Universe. Bereft of that divine instructor, man sees in everything around him, the necessity of a Creator, but sees not, that there is, and can be but one. In contemplating the stars, he believes that to every one of them, there is a separate creator, and from the moment that he admits a plurality of gods, he believes them all invested with absolute power, each within his separate jurisdiction, all constituted with human passions, good and bad; and all exercising a capricious and vindictive power, over the fortunes and destinies of mankind. He believes that there are two classes of creating gods one beneficent and the other malevolent or that they may be propitiated by flattery, and offended by neglect. He believes that they love justice, as he himself loves justice, when it suits his own interest, but that their love of justice, like his own, is warped by every selfish motive, and every groveling propensity which flesh is heir to. He believes that they are susceptible of sensual and of sordid impulses; that they are rivals in love and ambition, and that heaven is as discordant as earth a perpetual scene of civil wars, and insurrections, never totally suppressed. How deeply rooted in the human heart, are these radical errors, all flowing from the single false conception, that there can be more than one creator God, you may perceive in these lines of the most pious and orthodox, as well as the sublimest of modern poets.

For spirits when they please,
Can either sex assume, or both; so soft
And uncompounded is their essence pure,
Not ty'd or manacled with joint or limb,
Not founded on the brittle strength of bone,
Like cumbrous flesh; but in what shape they choose –
Dilated or condensed, bright or obscure,
Can execute their airy purposes,
And works of love or enmity fulfill.[25]

44 Works of love or enmity! He is speaking of those very deities, for whom the race of Israel often forsook the Lord Jehovah, the Creator and Ruler of the universe. When the mind and heart of man are perverted, to the belief

25 This is a quotation from John Milton's *Paradise Lost* – John Quincy Adams's favorite poem.

of first principles, such as these, the prevailing sentiment to which they are disciplined, in their relations with the spiritual world, and a future state, is base and servile fear. The gods are the very personification of earthly tyranny. If such a people commence a career of philosophical speculation, the first conclusion to which their free-thinkers will arrive, must be, that a multitude of creating gods, is an absurdity to which the free intellect cannot submit; and as the order of the universe is the most striking and most impressive of its properties, that a creation so orderly, and so invariably uniform in its operations, must, and can be, no other than the work of one Almighty mind. There is no doubt, that Thales, and Pythagoras, both came to that conclusion.

But the false gods, had priests, and worshipers, and shrines; and, from 45
the first moment, when the philosopher applies his lever and his screw, to the foundation of the temple of Dagon, he becomes the blasphemer of the gods, and his doom must be the bowl of hemlock, the fiery furnace, or the crucifix.

So it has been, in all ages, and in every region- And this is the reason 46
why Thales and Pythagoras, so carefully rolled up in profound mystery, all their discoveries in the moral and intellectual world.

At the restoration of the literature of Greece, and Rome, in the 47
fifteenth century, the great work of Ptolemy had perished in its original language. It existed, as a translation, in the Arabian Almagest, and was universally considered, as containing the only true system of the universe. It was then translated from the Arabic, into Latin, by Purbach and Muller, of Montreal, known according to the custom of that age, by the name of Regiomontanus. In commenting upon the translated work, they ventured to suggest some objections to the foundation of the system itself; that the earth was the center of the universe, and that, while she enjoyed perpetual repose, the sun, and moon, and all the planets of the solar system, from day to day, revolved round her. Shortly after wards, Nichola Copernicus dissolved the spell, restored the sun to his long prostrated supremacy, as the center of the system, and reduced the earth to her real station among the works of the Creator, as one of the smaller planetary satellites of the sun; while the sun himself, far from being the pre-eminent of nature, is, with his whole appendage of primary and secondary planets, and comets, no more than a relatively insignificant fragment of numberless similar systems, scattered over the regions of infinite space, and, for all we know, surpassing in

brightness, all the splendors of the sun, as far as they exceed the twinkling of a fire-fly.

48 The system of Copernicus, was so directly in the face of the testimony of the only sense, by which man can become acquainted with the stars, that, after he had made the discovery, and confirmed himself by observation and calculation, in the belief of its truth, he dared not publish it to the world.[26] Thirty years he kept it confined to his own bosom, or communicated it only to students, in the same science, on whose discretion and reserve, he could confidently rely. Independently of the difficulty, of reconciling mankind to the belief of a system of creation, contradictory to their senses, the revolution of the firmament, and the immobility of the. earth, had been taught as realities sanctioned by the Bible, and had be come articles of religious faith. To question them, was to cast a doubt upon the existence of the Creator, to deny the daily revolution of the sun, and moon, was to discredit the adjuration of Joshua, to them, to stand still for a single day. The Astronomer, at the peril of his liberty, or his life, must discover nothing which would require so much as an explanation of the meaning of a passage in Scripture ; and Copernicus, sensible that the truth is not always to be told, left the firmament to revolve, day by day, round the steadfast and immoveable earth, till, at the close of life, he permitted his system to be printed; but it was not published till after his death. Copernicus was born at Thorn, in Prussia, on the 19th of January, 1472, and died at Nuremburg, on the 25th of May, 1543, a few days after his work on the revolutions of the celestial orbs, had issued from the press.

49 Three years after his death, on the 13th of December, 1546, was born, in the Danish Island of Schonen, Tycho Brahe of the noble family of that name, illustrated by him as it had never been before. The study of Astronomy, kindled by the observation of an eclipse, in the tenth year of his age, was the passion of his life. He studied law, as a profession, at Leipsic, but his nightly vigils were occupied, not in poring over the Theodosian code, the compilations of Papinian, or the ponderous volumes of Cujacius, but in contemplating the majestic scenery of the heavens, and in tracing their courses and their causes, with that prying and pertinacious eagerness, which prompted his last words, repeatedly uttered, in the agonies of death,

26 Copernicus was Prussian polymath who first posited that the solar system revolves around the sun. The theory was later made famous by Galileo.

"Ne frustra vixisse videar."[27] The American mariner, or traveller, who passes from the North Sea into the Baltic, through the sound, between the Island of Zealand and the Swedish shore, as he approaches the Danish metropolis of Copenhagen, sees a small, seemingly solitary and deserted Island, close upon the Danish side of the strait, and will never fail to be told, there is the Island of Hueen there stood Uraniburg, the Observatory, built at his own expense, by Tycho Brahe, on a soil in which his sovereign, Frederick the Second, of Denmark, had granted him a life estate, and where, by twenty years of assiduous observation and study of the stars, he contributed his share, a large one, to open to his fellow man, the secret volume of creation, the mystery of the divine architect of the universe. Uraniberg is no longer there. It is of no human being the abode the owls, and the bats, have wrested it from the dominion of man. But there Tycho Brahe, and Kepler, served their country, and their kind, and its fame, as an appendage to theirs, shall be imperishable as the everlasting hills.

But the greatest flood of light, ever shed upon the science of Astronomy, 50
constitutes the unrivalled glory of the seventeenth century of the Christian era. The true founder of modern Astronomy, is acknowledged by Bailly, to be Kepler, born 27th December, 1571, at Wiel, in the dukedom of Wirtemberg; born of a noble, but decayed family, his father, after many years service as a captain in the military service of the king of Naples, was compelled, by poverty, to return to his native country, and there to follow the occupation of an innkeeper; and, even in that Condition, was unsuccessful, and fell into sordid indigence.[28] Young Kepler, was, therefore, bereft of all assistance from his parents, for his support, and cast upon his own resources, to provide for himself. Until his twentieth year, he studied divinity, at Tubingen, and became, for some time, a popular preacher. His teacher of mathe matics, Mobstlin, prevailed upon him, with no small repugnance, to devote himself to Astronomy. In the twenty-second year of his age, he was professor of mathematics, at Gratz, and published his first work, the Mysterium Commographicum; full of cabalistic fancies, concerning the recondite relations and mystic influence of proportional numbers. Throughout his life, he was in the habit of indulging in these day dreams, and was not a little

27 Adams' own translation of this Latin phrase is: "That I may not appear to have lived in vain."

28 Adams is here telling the story of the astronomer Johannes Kepler. He is most famous for his laws of planetary motions.

addicted to the practices of judicial Astrology. Yet, his first book introduced him to the acquaintance, and recommended him to the favor, of Tycho Brahe, by whose invitation, he went to him at Prague, and shortly before his death, was employed as his assistant, and obtained the office of mathematician to the emperor. Here he lived eleven years, in the most astringent penury, the small stipend of his office remaining unpaid. He then resided fifteen years, as professor of mathematics, at Linz ; three years afterwards, at Ulm, and one year, under the protection of the celebrated Wallenstein, at Sagan. He was repeatedly compelled to waste his time, in journeying, to obtain payment of his small pension, and, after passing the last year of his life at Rostock, in the exercise of his profession, died at Ratisbone, on the fifteenth of November, 1650, worn down with cares and affliction, leaving to his family, nothing but an imperishable name.

51 To the progress of Astronomical science, two distinct and separate operations of the mind are indispensable: observation and calculation. The first, requiring clear, keen, and distinct vision. This quickness of perception, is the gift of nature, and depends upon physical organization. This faculty is bestowed in a numberless variety of degrees; perhaps not the same, in any two of the human race. Ninety nine in a hundred of mankind, never look to heaven with a searching eye, and live the three score years and ten allotted to their existence, without knowing the difference, between a fixed star, and a planet. Among the labors of Astronomers, has been that of counting the numbers, and publishing the catalogues of all the stars, visible in the firmament, and to facilitate the operation, they have been divided into classes of graduated magnitudes. To the naked eye, of the great mass of mankind, no star of less than the fifth magnitude, can be seen. The favored few, endowed with more perfect optic nerves, can see stars of the sixth, and some, even of the seventh magnitude; and as every class exceed in number, those of all the preceding classes together, the portion of mankind invested with this faculty, has opened to the inspection of his senses, a second world, more populous than that which he enjoys, with the rest of mankind. Before the invention of the telescope, no mortal man had ever beheld a star of less magnitude, than the seventh; glasses are now constructed, which have revealed to the searching eye of the observer, hosts of heaven, down to the twelfth magnitude; and there is every reason to believe, that new accessions of light, will hereafter disclose millions upon millions of these luminaries, never yet seen by the eye of many. Copernicus, and Tycho Brahe, with all

the Astronomers of preceding ages, never saw a star not discernable to the naked eye. But the second operation of the mind, required for Astronomical discovery, is calculation, a talent acquired by study and intellectual labor, and increased wonderfully by long and pertinacious practice.

These two faculties, are sometimes but rarely possessed by the same 52
man, and not unfrequently has it happened, in the annals of Astronomy, that the observations of one man, fruitless, or but partially efficient to himself, have led to the most stupendous discoveries, by the calculations of another. Of this result, perhaps, the most memorable example, is presented in the joint and united labors of Tycho Brahe, and of Kepler. The transcendent merit of Tycho, consisted in the spirit with which he devoted his life, and an affluent fortune, to the cause of science, and the improvement of the condition of man. But, to turn to the most useful account, for the progress of Astronomical knowledge, the unparalleled mass of Tycho's observations, the powers of another, and kindred spirit, was indispensable; and that kindred spirit was found in the person of Kepler. The unanswerable demonstration of the Copernican discovery, that the central body of the solar system, is not the earth, but the sun, was contained in the recorded minutes of Tycho's observations, especially for a series of the movements for many months, of the planet Mars. But that demonstration, could be made manifest only by mathematical calculations. To this work, so far as mere readiness in the computation of numbers was required, Tycho was, no doubt, as competent as Kepler himself; but he was not restrained by religious scruples. The daily revolution of the sun round the earth, had not only been unquestioned in the Almagest of Ptolemy, for upwards of twelve hundred years, but was believed to be sanctioned by divine revelation, in the Bible. The religion of Tycho, in the encounter with his philosophy, obtained a triumph, honorable to him, but erroneous in fact. He rejected the great, and ever memorable discovery of Copernicus, and compounded a system of his own, more com plicated even than that of Ptolemy, whose epicycles he discarded, only to admit them again, because his own system could not be satisfactorily explained without them. Kepler had gone to live with Tycho, by his invitation, in the year 1600. In 1601, he died, and by that event, his observations on the planet Mars, fell into the hands of Kepler, who went to work upon them. The logarithms of Napier, were yet in the womb of time ten folio pages of multiplication, and division, and square, and cube roots, were covered with figures, by Kepler's hand; one error of

casting up, in this process, produced an erroneous result, and baffled the preconceived hopes of the calculator. The arithmetical computation was repeated: the error of the previous trial, was detected, and the result corresponded with the anticipations of the accountant. Seventy times over, was this process of calculation repeated, by the indefatigable hand of Kepler, and seven hundred folio pages of figures, attested the fact, that the motion of the planet Mars, in his orbit, was not circular, but elliptical, and that the sun was in one of the foci of that ellipsis. Subsequent calculations, on the movements of the other planets, confirmed the demonstration, as applicable to them, and settled forever the principle, that the sun is the center of the solar system; and that all the planets revolve round him, in elliptical orbits, in one focus of which, is his place.

53 The immense stride, in the progress of human knowledge, by the discoveries of Copernicus, and of Kepler, can be estimated only by the man, who, like them, can devote his time and his talents to the study of nature. Every human being can, and to some extent, does, observe the stars. To the eyes of all mankind, the sun and the firmament move from east to west, rising above the eastern horizon, every morning, and setting in the western horizon, at night. This is a false report to the human mind, made by the organ of observation, the human eye. The apparent movement of the sun, and stars, is occasioned by the real movement of the earth, rolling round her axis, and, like the ball of a bowling green, rolling on in an oval orbit, round the sun. The discovery of Copernicus, corrected this mistake. But to the eye of man, all the luminaries of the sky, large or small, appear round. He believes them to be spheres, and concludes, that, as they revolve, they must move in circles. The joint and several immense labors, of Tycho Brahe, and Kepler, resulted in the correction of this mistake, which Kepler communicated to the learned world, at Prague, in Bohemia, in a treatise, under the title of Celestial Physics, set forth in commentaries upon the movements of the star Mars, in the Latin language, in 1609.

54 The arcana of creation, were opened, by this work, to the inspection of man. Discoveries like these, are of a prolific nature. They breed with unparalleled exuberance. The discoveries and inventions of Kepler, would require the development of a volume, and your patience has already been strained, beyond the bounds of toleration.

55 The discoveries of Copernicus, and Kepler, disclosed, and corrected the mistakes of the optic nerve. But, in that same year, 1609, another invention,

not the effect of profound study and incessant labor, but of childish sport, and unforeseen casualty, gave new and increased powers to the orb of vision. James Metius, a mechanic, of the city of Alcmaer, in Holland, observed, on a winter's day, some school boys, sporting on the frozen canal, and adjusting fragments of the ice to the two ends of their ink-horns, and looking through them, to see the objects, at which they looked, With enlarged dimensions. Metius took the hint, and inserted into a wooden tube, an eye glass, at due focal distance from a double object glass, one convex, and the other concave, and presented one, as a sample of his invention, to the states general of the United Netherlands. The first use of these instruments was made by the navigators of the ocean; but one of Metius' spy glasses, having found its way to Venice, was seen there by Galileo Galilei, a native of Pisa, born on the 15th of February", 1564.

Galileo was, himself, one of the master spirits of his age, and of all 56
ages. The science of Astronomy, and the knowledge of the structure of the universe, is scarcely less indebted to him, than Copernicus, Tycho Brahe, or Kepler. To the ingratitude or neglect of the common herd of the rulers of mankind, suffered by all those benefactors of the race, he has the additional claim of the merit of martyrdom in their cause. At the very time when this new engine of discovery, the principle of the telescope, came to him like the present of a new pair of eyes, he was already involving himself in controversy, religious and philosophical, in support of the Copernican system, maintaining the central supremacy of the sun, and the subordinate revolutions of the planets round him. He immediately improved the spy glass of Metius into a telescope; let in a new flood of light upon the Astronomical observer's eye, and discovered by his own observation, several stars before unknown. The four satellites of Jupiter, the waxing and waning phases of the planets, Mercury and Venus, and the spots on the sun and moon. He was denounced, before the tribunal of the inquisition, and, in his own defence, wrote memoir upon memoir, to prevail upon the Pope, and the inquisitors, to declare the Copernican system, to be in strict conformity with the Holy Scriptures. As the Pope, and seven cardinals, appointed by him to solve this knotty question, pronounced, that the doctrine of the earth's motion, was an absurdity in physics, and a damnable heresy in religion, Galileo was expressly forbidden, ever again to maintain, by word of mouth, or in writing, that the rotary motion of the earth was countenanced by the holy scriptures. Cardinal Bellarmin, charged with the duty of announcing

this sentence to Galileo, gave him at the same time a certificate, that it was not pronounced, as a penalty; and that Galileo was not required, even to retract his opinions ; but was merely prohibitory, forbidding him from ever again maintaining it. He promised obedience, and observed it, for a period of thirty-seven years; when, in 1652, he published dialogues, to prove the immobility of the sun, and the planetary rotation of the earth round him. He was again summoned before the court of inquisition. Seven cardinals again pronounced his theory impious and absurd, and he was condemned, as a relapsed heretic, to three years' imprisonment, and to repeat the seven penitential psalms, once a week during that time.

57 At 70 years of age, Galileo was compelled by the sentence of these inquisitor cardinals, to crave pardon for having maintained the truth, and abjured it as absurdity, error and heresy, upon his knees, with his hands upon the gospel. With what spirit he per formed this ceremony, you may imagine, from the fact that, on ri sing from his knees, without raising his eyes from the ground, he stamped upon it, and said "Yet she moves!" He was finally discharged from prison, but in the last years of his life was afflicted with blindness, brought on by the intenseness of application to his telescope. He died at Florence on the 6th of January, 1641, and was buried in the Church of the Holy Cross; not without a long interval, during which his friends and admirers, desiring to erect a monument to his memory, by the side of that of Michael Angelo Buonarotti, were compelled to defer the execution of their purpose, till the popular prejudice against the apostle of truth, should have subsided into oblivion. In 1737, when it was no longer absurdity or sacrilege to believe, that the earth rolls round her axis, and round the sun, the monument was erected.

58 In the lives of Copernicus, of Tycho Brahe, of Kepler, and of Galileo, we see the destiny of almost all the great benefactors of mankind. We see, too, the irrepressible energies of the human mind, in the pursuit of knowledge and of truth, in conflict with the prejudices, the envy, the jealousy, the hatred, and the lawless power of their cotemporaries upon the earth. The institution, by the officers of which, Galileo suffered every persecution, short of death, which man could inflict upon him, was the invention of Ignatius Loyola, a man, in all the properties which constitute greatness, not inferior to Galileo himself. The profound meditation, the untamable activity, the untirable pertinacity, the unconquerable will, stiffening against resistance, overcoming obstacles, bearing down opposition, sweeping its

way along to its intended object, and, like faith, casting mountains into the sea, were alike in them both. What, then, was the difference between them? It was in the objects, to which they severally applied these properties, in action. Ignatius, under the influence of religious fanaticism, invents an engine of despotic power, a rod of iron, and puts it into the hands of a frail mortal man, already invested, by the infatuation of the age, with imputed infallibility. Galileo interrogates the physical creation, for the causes of its own existence, and his ultimate object, is the triumph of truth. To which of the contending causes must the voice of posterity say "God speed?" To the champion of truth and the truth shall ultimately prevail. But I may no longer dwell on the fascinating theme. Absorbed in the gigantic energies, and more than heroic labors of Copernicus, Tycho Brahe, Kepler, and Galileo, what time or space have I left, to speak to you of Newton, the consummation of them all; the man of whom, it was said, even by a cotemporary poet, with more than,

Nature, and nature's laws, lay hid in night,
God said, let Newton be, and all was light.[29]

The discoveries of Newton were so great, and so various, that a mere 59
enumeration of them would require a discourse too expansive, to be fitted for the present occasion. He was born at Woolstrope, in Lincolnshire, on Christmas day, O. S. 1642. His first essays' were in optics, the grinding of glass, and the theory of light. The magnifying, and approximating power of light, seen through a tube, and the medium of convex glass, had already become familiar, by the inventions of Metius and Galileo; but the changes of the nature of light, by reflection and refraction, in passing through glass, had not been made known, and DesCartes, one of the brightest geniuses of France, had published a treatise maintaining, that light was a simple and homogeneous substance. The papers upon light and optics, were first read to the Royal Society. They preceded khis mathematical principles of Natural Philosophy, published in 1687, containing his theory of the construction of the Universe, upon the principle and laws of gravitation.

It was the good fortune of Newton, to be born, and to live in a country, 60
where there was no college of Cardinals, to cast him into prison, and doom him to spend his days in repeating the seven penitential psalms, for shedding

29 The poet Alexander Pope on Newton.

light upon the world, and publishing mathematical truth. Newton was not persecuted by the dull and ignorant instruments of political, or ecclesiastical power. He lived in honor among his countrymen, was a member of one parliament received the dignity of knight-hood held for many years a lucrative office, and at his decease, was interred in solemn state, in Westminster Abbey, where a monument records his services to mankind, among the sepulchers of the British Kings. From the days of Newton, down to the present hour, the science of Astronomy has been cultivated, with daily, deepening interest, by all the civilized nations of Europe. The institutions of the Royal Society, and of the Greenwich Observatory in England, and of the Academy of Sciences, and of the Royal Observatory in Paris, have given to the study of the heavens, the dignity of schools, of which nations are the pupils. The example has been followed by Prussia, Sweden, several German, and several of the Italian states, and above all, by Russia, whose present soveregin, has made the pursuit of knowledge a truly imperial virtue. The skies of St. Petersburg, and of Moscow, are among the most unfavorable of the earth, for Astronomical observation; the perpetual snows of winter, and the perpetual daylight of summer, being equally unpropitious to that state of the atmosphere, in which, alone, the stars can be seen. But Astronomy, has always been one of the sciences, most assiduously cultivated, by the Academy of science, immediately under the inspection, and patronage of the Emperor. During the reign of Alexander, the Secretary of that Academy, was Schubert, the author of two systems of Astronomy, in the German language; one for the most learned in the science, and the other, for the common, popular reader; and hoth among the most perfect treatises upon the subject extant, in any language. At the University of Dorpat, there had long been an Astronomical Observatory, and in 1813, the observatory appointed to that edifice, was G. G. Struve, whose estimate of his duties in that capacity, is laid down in his own words, that he regards the duty of laboring for the progress of the science, which he cultivates, as the most important end of his existence. Thirty years of labors, invigorated by the spur of such motives, cannot have passed away, without results of the first importance; and Mr. Struve, is at this day, one of the most eminent Astronomers of the age.

61 In the seventeenth century, the invention of the telescope, gave to the Astronomical observer, a new sense for discovery in the heavens. In the latter part of the eighteenth century, the enlargement of the field of vision,

by increasing the size of the glasses, and the length of the telescopic tube, gave a new increase of power to the orb of human vision, and its first result was the discovery by the first Herschell, the inventor of the new tube, of a planet never before known, followed by many other subsequent discoveries, equally wonderful. And in the first half of the nineteenth century, a third enlargement of the visual orb, by object glasses of fourteen inches diameter, and tubes of twenty feet focal distance, unlocks again, the secret chambers of the firmament, finds a parallax in the bright star of Lyra, and exhibits solar systems of stars, revolving round each other, within limited space, by the hundred and the thousand.

The inventor of this instrument was Joseph Frauenhofer an ingenious 62
mechanic of Munich, in Bavaria. Did I say an ingenious mechanic? Rather, should I have said, one of those productions of nature, which once, in an age, she exhibits as symbols and samples of creative power. He was born at Straubing, in Bavaria, of parents so indigent, that they could not give him the education of a common school. His father was a glazier, and destined him to his own trade. But in his eleventh year he lost both his parents, and his guardian bound him for six years to a glass maker in Munich, without charge or compensation.

Towards the close of his apprenticeship, the house of his master, in 63
which he resided, fell in, and he was by a special interposition of Providence, and extraordinary exertions, encouraged by the personal presence and cheering of the king of Bavaria, drawn out uninjured from the ruin. The king of Bavaria, taking compassion at his misfortune, made him a present of eighteen ducates, with part of which, he purchased books upon optics, and with the rest, he bought from his master the last half year of his time. He was reduced to the necessity of engraving visiting cards for a subsistence, and struggling for years, at once for knowledge and for bread ; after many disappointments and disasters, he was at last admitted as a partner in the celebrated manufacturing establishment, for optical and mathematical instruments of Utzschneider and Reichenbach. From that time, the establishment soon acquired the reputation of the first optical instrument makers in Europe. Frauenhofer not only succeeded in making larger object glasses, than had ever been attempted, but by a composition of materials, known only to himself, he has made his glasses more perfect, for the transmission of light, than any that had ever been made before. In 1824, he furnished to Struve, for the University at Dorpat, the instrument which has

been called his great Achromatic Refractor, afterwards still more enlarged by a similar instrument, for the new Observatory of Pulkova. There, at this hour, perhaps, is Strove plying his optic nerve, to the detection of some never yet discovered wonder of the firmament, with an object glass of fourteen inches aperture, a tube of twenty-one feet focal distance, and a magnifying power of two thousand fold duplication.

64 With the great Achromatic Refractor of Dorpat, Struve has been from the year 1824, constantly observing the most interesting phenomena of the heavens. His observations upon the moon, upon the planet Saturn, and upon many other celestial objects, have been of the most interesting character. But the great and transcendent labors of Struve, have been concentrated upon the ascertainment of the numbers and properties of the double, treble and quadruple stars, of which, at three several periods, he has published catalogues. Of the labors incident to these operations, some estimate may be formed, by reflecting on the fact, that in the space of two years and a half, the passage of the meridian was noted of one hundred and twenty thousand stars, from the first to the eighth magnitude. That three thousand one hundred and twelve of those stars, were ascertained to be double stars. Eleven years of these observations were consumed with inferior instruments, and twelve years with the great refractor of Frauenhofer. They are not yet completed.

65 The discovery of a new planet, by the elder Herschel, in 1781, was an electric spark in the atmosphere of Astronomy. In compliment to his royal patron, George the third, he called it the Georgium Sidus. The learned Astronomers of Europe, for some time, moved by an impulse of gratitude to the finder, gave it his name, and called it Herschel. The classical taste of the German scholars, following the analogy of the names given to the ancient planets, called it Uranus, which denomination, has finally prevailed, and been followed, by naming the four further discovered planets, Juno, Vesta, Ceres and Pallas discoveries, the merit of which, may be ascribed to Herschel, as if he had been the first to see them himself.[30]

66 The new impulse given by this glorious achievement, of Herschel, to the study of physical Astronomy, pervaded all Europe. The class of observers was multiplied, and their visual organs were quickened; Observatories started up in every quarter, like the enchanted castles of romance. Is it not

---

30 Juno, Ceres, and Pallas are minor planets that are no longer considered full planets like Uranus.

strange, that the spark of enthusiasm never crossed the Atlantic? That the star of empire, then streaming like a Comet, in her western course, should not have been outstripped by the star of science; or at least, have illuminated, with double splendor, the path of the star of power?

The discovery of Herschel, was made in 1781, amid the fiercest flames 67
of the war of independence. The new nation entered upon the magnificent scene of sovereign, independent potentates, with a progression of principles, elevating the standard of human virtue, to its highest pitch of perfection. She announced herself as the friend and patroness of science; she proposed to her sisters, of the European world, the abolition of war upon the Ocean, forever. Her Congress issued proclamations of peace and protection, to the English navigator of discovery, when winding his way round the globe, upon the seas. How, and why was it, that she seems to have received in sullen, if not in envious silence, the annunciation of that sublime discovery, of a new planet, added to the glory of God, in the works of creation; at the sound of which, the whole learned world of Europe shouted and clapped their hands for joy.

The theme is painful - let me pass it over. Not such, was the influ- 68
ence upon the youthful mind of Nicholas, the imperial autocrat of all the Russias, of the new discoveries in the region of the stars, accomplished by the genius of Frauenhofer, and the never ceasing vigilance and untiring penetration of Struve. Not a year has passed away since the great refractor of Frauenhofer. has been the instrument in the hand of Struve, without bringing to light some new phenomena, interesting to the progress of science. The promotion of knowledge has wound itself into the heart of the Academy of Sciences, of the minister of public instruction, of the Emperor Nicholas himself.

Besides the Observatory at Dorpat, there had been, from the time of 69
the institution by Peter the Great, of the Academy of Sciences, at St. Petersburg, an Astronomical Observatory, connected with it there. Similar establishments had, in later days, been erected at Abo afterwards transferred to Helsingfors at Nicolaief, on the Black Sea at Moscow Kasan and Kiew. Various causes had combined to render these institutions inefficient, and the tower in the city of St. Petersburg was unfavorably situated for the purposes of observation. The heights of Pulkova, between St. Petersburg and Zarsko Zelo, had long been noticed as admirably situated for erecting upon them an Observatory, and when the results of the use of Frauenhofer's

great refractor at Dorpat began to ring in the public ear, the Emperor Nicholas commanded a plan to be prepared, and presented to him, for an Observatory of the first class, to be erected there.

70 A plan was accordingly prepared in April, 1834, with estimates of the expense required for the erection of the building, and for the purchase of suitable instruments for observation; the first amounting to 346,500 rubles, and the second to 135,000 rubles the value of the ruble being 74 cents of our currency. The Emperor immediately issued an order to commence the work, under the direction of three commissioners, members of the academy; and that 100,000 rubles should be placed at the disposal of the minister of public instruction, for the prosecution of the work. It was accordingly commenced, vigorously prosecuted, and finally completed; at a cost of little less than one million of rubles; and the Observatory of Pulkova, has been, for years, the most magnificent and best appointed establishment, for the observation of the heavens, in the world.

71 Of this truly imperial munificence, much must undoubtedly be ascribed, to the generous and liberal spirit of the Emperor Nicholas; but, after all, it is but an exemplification of the spirit of the age. Of such exemplifications, the annals of European science are full. They are manifested, in the number of Astronomical Observatories, illuminating every part of the European continent in the number of eminent observers, stationed at those watch-towers of science, in those cotemporaneous discoveries of three planets at Bremen, in Germany, and another at Palermo, in Sicily, in the number of periodical publications, devoted to the continual development of the phenomena of the heavens, in the advances to perfection, in the theory of the science from the solar centralism of Copernicus, and the planetary laws of Kepler, and the gravitation of, Newton, to the celestial mechanism of La Place, and its improved revisal of our own Bow- ditch. Finally, in the institution of Astronomical societies, and particularly that in our mother country, within the last quarter of a century, blooming in youth, and already bearing, from year to year, fragrant and delicious fruits, for the harvest of the human mind.

72 But what, in the meantime, have we been doing? While our fathers were colonists of England, we had no distinctive, political, or literary character. The white cliffs of Albion, covered the soil of our nativity, though another hemisphere first opened our eyes to the light of day, and oceans rolled between us and them. We were Britons born, and we claimed to be

the countrymen of Chaucer and Shakespeare, Milton and Newton, Sidney and Locke, Arthur and Alfred, as well as of Edward, the black Prince, Harry, of Monmouth, and Elizabeth. But when our fathers abjured the name of Britons, and "assumed among the powers of the earth, the separate and equal station, to which the laws of Nature, and of Nature's God, entitles them," they tacitly contracted the engagement for themselves, and above all, for their posterity, to contribute, in their corporate and national capacity, their full share; aye, and more than their full share, of the virtues, that elevate, and of the graces that adorn the character of civilized man. They announced themselves, as reformers of the institution of civil society. They spoke of the laws of Nature, and in the name of Nature's God; and by that sacred adjuration, they pledged us, their children, to labor with united and concerted energy, from the cradle to the grave, to purge the earth of all slavery to restore the race of man, to the full enjoyment of those rights, which the God of Nature, had bestowed upon him at his birth to disenthrall his limbs from chains to break the fetters from his feet, and the manacles from his hands, and to set him free, for the use of all his physical powers, for the improvement of his own condition. The God, in whose name they spoke, had taught them, in the revelation of his gospel, that the only way in which man can discharge his duty to him, is, by loving his neighbor as himself, and doing with him, as he would be done by, respecting his rights, while enjoying his own, and applying all his emancipated powers of body, and of mind, to self-improvement, and improvement of his race.

Among the modes of self-improvement, and social happiness, there is 73
none so well suited to the nature of man, as the assiduous cultivation of the arts and sciences. The opportunities and dispositions of individuals, for the cultivation of any one specific art or science, are infinitely diversified. One general impulse nerves the arm, and animates the soul, but, in giving direction to that impulse, everyone may best follow the bent of his own inclination. We have been sensible of our obligation to maintain the character of a civilized, intellectual, and spirited nation. We have been, perhaps, over boastful of our freedom, and over sensitive to the censure of our neighbors. The arts and sciences, which we have pursued with most intense interest, and persevering energy, have been those most adapted to our own condition. We have explored the seas, and fathomed the depths of the ocean, and we have fertilized the face of the land. We have converted the wilderness into a garden, and opened a paradise upon the wild. But have not the

labors of our hands, and the aspirations of our hearts, been so absorbed in toils upon this terraqueous globe, as to overlook its indissoluble connection even physical, with the firmament above? Have we been of that family of the wise man, who, when asked where his country lies, points, like Anaxagoras. with his finger to the heavens.

74 Suffer me to leave these questions unanswered. For, however chargeable we may have been, with inattention or indifference, to the science of Astronomy, heretofore, you, fellow citizens, of Cincinnati you, members of the Astronomical Society, of this spontaneous city of the West, will wipe that reproach upon us, away. That edifice, of which, under your charge, the cornerstone is now to be laid, will rise, a lasting monument of your ardent and active zeal, to connect the honor of your country, with the constant and untiring exploration of the firmament of heaven; and may the blessing of Him, who, from his lofty throne, rules the universe in wisdom and goodness, crown your labors with success

Chapter 5:
On The History of New England
(1843)

In honor of the two-hundredth anniversary of the formation of the United Colonies of New England (an organization usually just called the New England Confederation), the Massachusetts Historical Society commissioned John Quincy Adams to deliver an essay on the history and legacy of the Confederacy. Adams took this as an opportunity to discuss first the unique religious and cultural past of the region he called home, before laboriously detailing the inner workings of the Confederacy itself. The New England Confederacy lasted only forty years, though it did provide England's most northeastern colonies with an adequate method of self-defense against Native American and Dutch attacks. However, in a deeper sense, Adams condemns the Confederacy as a failure. He argues that since its collapse the unique culture of New England has been gradually eclipsed by a larger American ethos tied to the national regime his family helped forge. Yet in America, Adams observes the ultimate triumph of his New England forefathers. Theirs was a regime founded on the "natural equality of mankind" – an outlook that has found its next champion not in quiet New England villages but in the majestic march of the United States of America.

My breathern of the Massachusetts Historical Society, fellow citizens, laides 1
and gentlemen.

In reviewing the history of this confederated Union, one of the first 2
remarks which impresses itself on the mind of the philosophical observer, is the heterogeneous and conflicting primitive elements of which it was composed. It has been said that the most essential qualifications for a historian are to have neither religion nor country. And if religion consisted of a blind, unquestioning zeal in support of speculative dogmas transmitted from generation to generation, under the seal of a fisherman's ring, and the infallible dictate of a fallible man; if patriotism were compounded of the mere impulse of passion to support right or wrong, the purposes of the land in which you were born, or the community to which you belong, - then

indeed the devout worshipper and the ardent patriot must discard all the emblems of his religion and his country, before he may dare to assume the pen of the historian.

3 History is the record of the transactions of human beings associated in communities — not of all their transactions, because there are multitudes of human actions which neither the actor nor any other of his fellow creatures can have any possible interest in remembering; and other greater multitudes which the interest of the actor and of all others, requires to be buried in oblivion. But whatever in the transactions of associated man bears on the causes and motives of their congregation into communities, and on their corporate existence and well being, assumes the character of a material for history. The history of the United States of America commenced with a bloody revolution and a seven years war, which separated a part of them from the condition of colonies, subject to the sovereignty of the crown of England, from which they had received their charters. These charters as *colonies* gave them no right, either to dissolve their allegiance to their common sovereign beyond the seas, or to form any confederation or alliance between themselves, much less to constitute themselves one peo ple. This complicated and transcendent act of sovereignty was and could be performed only by the people themselves, through their representatives. As representatives of the colonies, they could have no right to dissolve their allegiance; as representatives of the colonies they could exercise only delegated power, and the colonies themselves had no power either to dissolve their own allegiance or to form a new social compact constituting a new sovereign authority over them all. By the dissolution of their ties and oaths of allegiance they dissolved also their connection with their country. They were no longer British subjects. They renounced all claim of protection from the government of Great Britain. They held and declared they held the people of Great Britain no longer as countrymen, fellow subjects or fellow citizens, but as the rest of mankind, enemies in war; in peace friends."

4 Their union de facto had existed from the time of the first meeting of the Congress at Philadelphia, in September ber, 1774; but that union had been formed, not by chartered rights, but by the primitive, natural rights of man, revolutionary and transcendental: The inalienable right of resistance to oppression - the right bestowed by the God of nature, preceding all human association, to dissolve a government which fails to discharge the duties for which all governments are instituted; and the resulting right to

form and establish a new government to supply the place of that which had been dissolved. This dissolution of allegiance was thus proclaimed by the whole people of these North American colonies, and with the dissolution of the common allegiance, they declared the colonies free and independent states. They thereby reconferred upon the colonial governments all the authorities, which by the charters of the several colonies they had possessed, and without forming one general government for the whole people, left to the people of each several state, the right of forming for themselves a state constitution, and proceeded to form for the whole a confederation of separate and independent states.

The revolutionary union still continued. The people of the several states 5
formed and established their separate state constitutions. Four years of time were consumed in the painful and laborious preparation, by the joint agency of the general congress, and of the state legislatures of a confederation, which, when adopted, proved to be a body without a soul- a marble statue, without Promethean fire. The whole people of the Union were taught by severe experience, that what they wanted was a common government, and that a confederacy is not a government. They commenced their work again as one people, and formed the constitution of the United States -- a government under which more than one generation of men have already lived and passed away; and which, with the blessing of divine Providence, we may yet hope will prove a bond of union to this great and growing nation, for untold ages yet to At this time its most imminent dangers arise, not from external aggression, but from its prospects and temptations to aggrandizement. The territories which originally constituted the domain of the North American Union, already so extensive at the time when the constitution was under the consideration of the people, as to constitute one of the most formidable objections against its adoption, have since that period been more than doubled, by the acquisition and annexation of Louisiana and the Floridas. With the expansion of the surface of soil, to be cultivated and replenished by the swarming myriads of our future population, men of other races, the children of other blood, bred to other opinions, accustomed to other institutions, trained to other prejudices, and disciplined to other principles, have been invested with the community of our rights, and mingled with the tide of our common concerns. It was by the accession of foreign conquered nations to the rights and privileges of Roman citizens, that the republic degenerated into an empire, and the empire itself

was overrun and extinguished by hordes of foreign barbarians. The people of the United States themselves, who declared and achieved their independence, were not all of one common origin. The United Netherlands, Sweden, Germany, the refugees from religious persecution in France, had contributed to the still scanty streams of population covering the broad surface of the thirteen colonies at the time of their political revolution. In the origin of the colonies which united to achieve their independence, the most opposite and discordant elements were combined. All the parties, religious and political, which for more than two centuries, had convulsed and desolated the mother country, were now united in harmony against her. The cavalier of the court of Charles the First had begun the settlement of Virginia, though the name of the colony dated back to the romantic age of Elizabeth. The rigid Roman Catholic nobleman of Ireland formed the adjoining settlement to that of Virginia; while, at a later period, the aristocratic republic of John Locke at the south, and the hereditary quaker monarchy of William Penn at the north, bordered upon the settlements of Virginia and Maryland. Next to these, Sweden, in the days of Christina, and the United Netherlands, emancipated from the dominion of Spain, had commenced establishments destined to fall at an early day, by the right of conquest, into the hands of the Anglo Saxon. The spirit of adventure in France had already penetrated to those Mediterranean seas, which seem to be but the overflowing of the river St. Lawrence, and to the hyper borean skies of Acadia.

6 The first English colony upon this continent, had received from the Virgin Queen, even before its birth, the name, now so illustrious, of Virginia. By her immediate successor, James the First, there was granted a territory from the thirtieth to the forty-eighth degree of latitude, to two companies of merchants, one residing in London and the other at Plymouth, so that the benefits of the trade for which those companies were incorporated, might be shared alike by the inhabitants of the east and west of England. The London company, by its location in the metropolis of the kingdom, possessed of course more means and larger resources, and obtained, in point of settlement, the start of the other. But the same John Smith, who had been so distinguished in the settlement of Virginia, had in 1614 visited for purposes of trade, the northern division of the territory, and gave, on his return to England, so flattering an account of the country, that Charles the First, then Prince of Wales, gave to it, as a token of his

favor, the name of New *England*, which thenceforward superseded that of Virginia;- New England, a name still dear to our remembrance, as a link of connection with the land of our forefathers , and of which,I trust, neither we nor our successors to the latest generation will ever have reason to be ashamed. It is a name peculiarly appropriate to that portion of the territory of this Union which yet bears it, and to the people by whom it is inhabited. The name of Yankee, some times given to them in derision, was, in its origin, but the Indian pronunciation of the word *English*, and whoever may at any time incline to couple it with a sarcasm or a sneer, it is the genuine representative of many of the noblest qualities that elevate and adorn the human character. As citizens of the great community, we may cordially greet as fellow citizens, all whom the constitution and the laws entitle, of whatever lineage or descent, and whether entitled to them by birth or by adoption; but the name of New England carries with it a code of moral and religious principles, embedded in the seminal institutions of our pilgrim fathers of Plymouth and Massachusetts, pure from the fountain of human rights, gathered from the intermingling streams of *English* liberty, and as yet uncontaminated by any the remotest taint of slavery. New England is the child of that puritan race, whom David Hume, with extorted reluctance, acknowledges to have been the founders of all the liberties of the English nation. "So powerful, " says Dr. Robertson "is the attraction of our native soil, and such our fortunate partiality to the laws and manners of our own country, that men seldom choose to abandon it unless they be driven away by oppression, or allured by vast projects of sudden wealth; " and again, "something more than the prospect of distant gain to themselves, or of future advantages to their country, was requisite in order to induce men to abandon the place of their nativity, to migrate to another quarter of the globe, and endure innumerable hardships under an untried climate, and in an uncultivated land covered with woods, or occupied by fierce and hostile tribes of savages. But what mere attention to private emolument or to national utility could not effect, was accomplished by the operation of a higher principle. Religion had gradually excited among a great body of the people, a spirit that fitted them remarkably for encountering the dangers and surmounting the obstacles which had previously rendered abortive the schemes of colonization in that part of America allotted to the company of Plymouth." He proceeds to remark, that the various settlements in New England are indebted, for their origin, to this spirit, and that in the course of his narrative, would be discerned its influence, mingling in all their transactions, giving a peculiar tincture to the character of the people, as well as to their institutions, both civil and ecclesiastical.

7 The primary cause then of the various settlements of New England was religion. It was not the search for gold — it was not the pursuit of wealth — it was not the spirit of adventure. It was not the martial spirit of conquest, which animated our English forefathers to plant themselves here in a desert and barren wilderness, to lay the foundations of the mightiest empire that the world ever saw. It was religion. It was the Christian religion, purified and refined from its corruptions, by the fires of persecution. The first colonists were indeed of that class of emigrants from their native land, driven away by oppression; but in the settlements of Plymouth and of Massachusetts, the stern and severe impulses of religion were tempered by the tenderest and most attractive sympathies of *English patriotism*. The Plymouth colonists had been fugitives from the north of England, who from time to time had escaped by crossing the North Sea to Holland, in numbers sufficient to form an English church at Leyden. They had fled from their country for the enjoyment of religious liberty in peace. But with that religion was inseparably connected the code of Christian morals in its simplicity and in its purity — a code above all others resting upon the fundamental principle of the natural equality of mankind. The English puritan found in Holland a refuge from the persecution of his own countrymen, but he found not his English home, he found not the same system of pure morals to which his soul was bound. In the lapse of time, he found that his children were leaving him and losing the name of Englishmen: and notwithstanding all that he had suffered from the injustice of his countrymen, so intense was his attachment to the name of England, that interdicted as he was from returning to her bosom, he determined to seek, beyond the Atlantic Ocean, at the distance of three thousand miles, in the most desolate region of the new hemisphere, a spot of earth where he could make for himself an English home, and find or create in the wilderness a New England, as the only consolation accessible to his heart for the loss of the Old. The same spirit is breathed in the address from the company of the Massachusetts colony, dated at Yarmouth, on the 7th of April, 1630, on board of the Arbella. In the fervent spirit at once of piety and of patriotism, they earnestly beseech their countrymen whom they leave behind, to consider them as their brethren, needing their prayers for the successful

accomplishment of their great and arduous undertaking; professing not to be of those that dream of perfection in this world, they yet desire their countrymen to take notice of the principals and body of their company, as those who esteem it their honor to call *the church of England*, from whence they rose, their dear mother, and could not part from their native country, where she especially resided, without much sadness of heart and many tears in their eyes. In these recorded monuments of the motives which prompted the pilgrims both of the Plymouth and of the Massachusetts colonies, in their emigration to this hemisphere, may we not clearly discern the peculiar propriety with which the name of New *England* was given to the land which they were to inhabit? The profound sense of their duty to God — the tender tie of affection for their native land the puritan *moral* principle of equal and inalienable rights — the secret, pungent and only spur to their secession from that dear mother church, whom they so dearly loved, and yet from whom with such agonizing tears they were compelled to part! Oh! how was it possible that this combination of elementary principles, swelling with an irresistible impulse to action in the bosoms of our patriarchal forefathers, could be so signally manifested and so deeply rooted in the hearts of all their posterity, and in the memory of all mankind, as by adopting for their country in the new world, the name of that which had been the center of all their affections in the old.

In all the colonial establishments of the European world in this hemi- 8
sphere, there was a question of right by the laws of nature and of nature's God, which met the European adventurer as he landed upon the shore — the proprietary right of the prior occupant. By the law of nature, independent of all revelation, and by the concurrent testimony of holy writ in the narrative of the creation, the earth was given by the Creator to the family of man, for the purpose of improving the condition of its possessor, and power was given them over the lives of all other animals on the surface or in the bowels of the earth, in the bosom of the waters or suspended in the sky.[1] The Scripture says they were all given to man as articles of food - but no such power was given over his brother man. As the exclusive possession of the portion of the earth occupied by man for tillage must be held by

1 John Quincy Adams is referring to Genesis 1:26: "Then God said, 'Let us make man in our image, after our likeness. And let them have dominion over the fish of the sea and over the birds of the heavens and over the livestock and over all the earth and over every creeping thing that creeps on the earth.'"

the occupant, at least for a season, the right of exclusive property becomes vested — by the law of nature the *right* of the first occupant, and by the continuous labor of tillage from season to season, that exclusive proprietary right becomes permanent, and includes the right of enclosure and of exclusion of all other occupants. Unoccupied earth may be used by man for the pursuit of those animals given him by the Creator, for food or for pastime: but the earth cannot be used at once for the purposes of the chase and of tillage; which cannot be commenced on any given portion of earth, until the animal occupants of its soil have been expelled. The European settlers on the territories included within the bounds of New England, came from their transatlantic homes as tillers of the earth. They came to hold the earth for tillage, and of course for exclusive possession. They found the country occupied by tribes of wandering savages without permanent habitation, without exclusive occupation, using the ground not for tillage, but for hunting, and having therefore, no exclusive right to the soil. The Indian savage used the earth only to range over its surface in search for prey.[2] The European settler needed it for permanent and exclusive possession by tillage. These rights could not subsist together. By the law of nature the right of each party was subject to the condition of operating no wrong to the other. The Indian savage was bound to renounce his right of hunting on so much of the ground as was necessary to the European settler for tillage, and the European was bound to make a reasonable compensation to the Indian, for the extinction forever, of his right of hurting on those identical grounds. But the Indian hunter had no permanent right to the soil to renounce, and the European settler did him no wrong by assuming, after compensating him for his right of hunting there, exclusive possession of the soil to himself. Of the European settlers on the American continent, the colonists of New England were the first who ever held themselves bound to respect the right of prior occupancy of the Indian savage and to purchase it of him for an equivalent. But the Indian could grant no more than he possessed, and with the exception of his wigwam , which had no permanent location, his only right was to hunt and fish within certain determinate metes and bounds. The whole territory of New England was thus purchased for valuable consideration by the new comers, and the Indian title was extinguished

2 Though typically quite enlightened on issues of race, Adams is here spouting the largely discredited view that Native American civilization was entirely migratory and never settled upon land in any significant way.

by compact fulfilling the law of justice between man and man. The most eminent writer on the Law of Nations, of modern times, Vattel, has paid a worthy tribute of respect to our forefathers, for their rigid observance in this respect of the natural rights of the indigenous natives of the country. It is from the example of the New England puritans that he draws the preceptive rule, and he awards to them merited honor for having established it.

My Brethren of the Massachusetts Historical Society, the reputation of 9
our forefathers is the choicest inheritance and the richest possession they have left us. The preservation of their good name from those slanders with which they were so bitterly persecuted, and so pertinaciously assailed in their own time, and which, passing from age to age, with a perseverance of envy and detraction, are yet showered upon them, is one of the preëminent duties of our Society. If justice rules the ball - if communities are accessible to the chastisements of future retribution, there is a fearful account of wrong, of which the civilized white European will be responsible hereafter, to the Indian races of this hemisphere, for the balance. Nor is the account yet closed. We ourselves assembled here, are yet witnessing, in silent acquiescence, a treatment of the Indian tribes cursed with our protection by the government of our national Union - a treatment marked with perfidy as faithless, with oppression as grievous, with tyranny as inexorable as ever presided over the conquests of Cortes or Pizarro.[3] The history of our negotiations for the last ten or twelve years with the Indian tribes, and their result, present in sad relief the expulsion of the southern tribes, not only from their hunting grounds but from their own domain; from the possession of the soil acquired by their conversion at our instance and under our persuasion, from the hunter to the agricultural state. From their planted lands - from their comfortable dwellings - from their domestic hearths, and the sepulchers of their fathers, pledged by solemn treaties to their perpetual possession, they have been expelled by the rude hand of violence, and driven like herds of cattle, to a common receptacle beyond the Mississippi, whence they are already threatened again with expulsion, by their neighbors of Arkansas and Missouri.

3 Here Adams is referring to the Indian removal policies of Andrew Jackson and his successors. The Indian removal forcibly removed the five largest tribes remaining east of the Mississippi to Oklahoma. It was soon followed by the cruel conquest of the western United States and the tribes who lived there. That conquest was undertaken by the US government and by settlers who moved in droves west of the Mississippi in the early and late nineteenth century.

10 It is not for us, therefore, to charge with injustice or cruelty towards the original inhabitants of this continent, the puritan English colonists of the seventeenth century. The transition of an extensive region of the globe, from a land of hunters to a land of planters, is the metamorphosis of a wilderness into a garden. How pleasing to the imagination is the scene — and yet how afflicting to the sense of humanity, the process of the operation! The tenant of the wilderness must be dispossessed or withdraw; the game which furnishes at once his subsistence and the occupation of his life must be exterminated; flocks and herds of tame animals must take the place of the beaver, the buffalo, and the deer, and the tassels of the maize, the waving grass, the bean - pole and the pea - vine, must open their ripening fruits to the sun, on ground hidden even from the face of the hunter by tangled thickets, and gnarled oaks, and enormous hemlocks in thick array, standing as if in defiance of the genial influence of the sky. Yet, by some mysterious law of nature, man the hunter, becomes, in the process of time, so attached to his condition that he inflexibly refuses to change it; he perseveres in his roving pursuits of the chase; he refuses to erect for himself a permanent habitation; he neither tills the ground, nor attempts to tame the beasts of the field, nor the fowls of the air for his use: he has no genius for the mechanic arts; he has no relish for sedentary labors: he borrows occasionally from the civilized man, a blacksmith to sharpen his tools, and exchanges his prey from the chase, for the rifle, the powder, and the ball, more expeditious, for his own work of destruction, than his bow and arrow. He is formed for the wilderness, and the wilderness is formed for him.

11 The confederation of which this day is selected as the two hundredth anniversary, was formed between the four New England colonies of Plymouth, Massa chusetts, Connecticut, and New Haven. The date of the act of confederation itself, is the 19th of May, 1643; it was then subscribed at Boston, where it had been negotiated, by Increase Howell, secretary of the general court of Massachusetts, by John Haynes and Edward Hopkins, commissioners from Connecticut, and by Theophilus Eaton and Thomas Gregson, from New Haven. The commissioners from Plymouth were Edward Winslow and William Collier; but although the confederation itself had originated in that colony, and had been first proposed by her, she had not authorized her commissioners to conclude, without reference back to her own general court, which was done, and at the second meeting of the commissioners, held at Boston in September of the same year, the

commissioners from Plymouth presented an order of their general court of 29th August, 1643, attesting that the articles of confederation were read, approved, and confirmed by the said court and all their townships, and their commissioners authorized to ratify them by their subscriptions, which they accordingly did on the 7th of September, 1643.

The parties to this confederacy were the colonies, 1st, of Plymouth; 2d, 12
of Massachusetts; 3d, of Connecticut; 4th, of New Haven. 1st, *The Plymouth Colony* is remarkable for having furnished the first example in modern times of a social compact or system of government instituted by voluntary agreement, conformably to the laws of nature, by men of equal rights, and about to establish their permanent habitation as a community in a new country. Upon their landing at Plymouth in the dead of winter, they had no charter from their king and no right to the soil upon which they landed.

The grants of rights and powers for the exercise of colonial governments 13
in the colonies were in that age exercised by the kings of England. It was a branch of the royal prerogative, assumed but never legalized. The right of conquering distant lands inhabited by infidels, had grown an absurd and unnatural excrescence from the conversion of Constantine to the Christian faith.[4] The words he had heard in his nightly vision of a crucifix surrounded with celestial splendors, in this conquer: In this conquer;- and the imposture itself of that pretended miracle affords evidence superabundantly that the impulse of Constantine to embrace the *Christian* religion, was not the adorable doctrines and heavenly precepts of the meek and lowly Jesus, but worldly grandeur, imperial power, and dominion on the earth. The despotism of imperial Rome engrafted upon the hierarchy of the church, formed the system substituted for that of *human rights* under which mankind has groaned from the age of the Cæsars to this day. Jesus Christ had said to the Apostle Peter; " Thou art a rock, and upon this rock I will build my church, and the gates of hell shall not prevail against it. And I will give unto thee the keys of the kingdom of heaven: and whatsoever thou shalt bind on earth shall be bound in heaven; and whatsoever thou shalt loose on earth shall be loosed in heaven." Whatever power was conferred upon Peter by these words, it is subject to two restrictive conditions. First, the kingdom, the keys of which were promised to Peter, was not of this world. It was no grant of temporal power. And secondly, it was a grant exclusively to Peter,

4 Adams is referring to the Emperor Constantine – the first Roman emperor to convert to Christianity.

without any authority to him to devolve the same upon any other person, much less authorizing others to confer it upon his successors. Yet upon this airy foundation the church of Rome erected the most stupendous and unlimited engine of power, spiritual and temporal, that ever weighed upon the family of man, For the successors of Saint Peter assumed that all the kingdoms of the earth were to be made kingdoms of heaven, and that the persons and property of all nations not already subjected to Christianity, were, by this donation of Jesus to Peter, placed at their absolute and arbitrary disposal. One of the most prominent exercises of this power was the Bull of Alexander, the 6th of May, 1494, granting to Ferdinand and Isabella of Spain all the lands west of a line drawn from the south pole, one hundred leagues west of the Azores and Cape de Verd Islands.

14 When the kings of England seceded from the authority of the church of Rome they substituted themselves as heads of the church , and assumed all the authority over foreign and barbarous nations for the purpose of converting them to Christianity, which had been assumed at any time by the bishops of Rome. They also *granted* the lands of foreign and barbarous nations (as were all those of the western hemisphere) without any restriction whatever in the exercise of power over their persons or their property. They held their own subjects engaged in such enterprises always and everywhere inalienably bound in allegiance to them and declared them always and everywhere entitled to their sovereign protection. None of these transcendental and elementary questions of relative *right* and *power* between the sovereign and the subject, and between the European adventurer and the indigenous native of America, appear to have arisen in the formation of any other colonies than those of New England.

15 The Pilgrims of Plymouth landed on a desert within the boundaries assigned by the charter of Charles the First to the Plymouth company; but they came not with license from the company itself. They came not even as English subjects, but as strangers, long exiled from her borders by the tyranny of her laws, seeking a place of refuge under the protection of another sovereign, but cast again by an accident, over which they had no control, upon the tender mercies of that ecclesiastical power from which they had already found no salvation but by escaping from their country. Without the shadow of blame upon themselves, and in the exercise of the purest energies that can direct and guide the conduct of men, they were outlawed both from England and from the Netherlands; and the social

compact, signed on the deck of the Mayflower before their landing, was the necessary result of their situation as men in a state of nature, subject to no law but that which they consented to impose upon themselves.

In the establishment of the Massachusetts colony, an incident had 16
occurred which, whether intended by those who proposed and accomplished it, or merely projected for the special convenience of the emigrants and afterwards accommodating itself to their condition and wants so as silently to effect a revolution, did certainly change the whole system of English colonization, and by bestowing upon the colonies themselves an organization perperpetually tending to independence, gradually predisposed the minds and measures of men to that final separation from the parent stock which it was impossible not to foresee must, in the lapse of ages, prove unavoidable. I speak of the transfer of the charter itself to America. Certainly nothing like this could have been contemplated in the original establishment of the company. That was instituted for purposes of trade, and of which the adventurers, who furnished the funds, would naturally choose to retain the management in their own hands. The charter transferred to America was a constitution of government, and as such was always considered. It left the liberties and the actions of the settlers in the new country entirely under their own control, released from the humors and prejudices of a court of directors in London. Under that management it would necessarily have followed that all the measures of the corporation would have been taken with final reference to the interests of the undertakers at home. It would have been a company to be enriched, and not a people to be governed. The change was a total one, a democratic revolution. By the transfer of the charter to America, the management of the affairs of a joint stock trading company. by its members, was changed into the government of a people –a pure democracy - and in the space of four years after the landing of John Winthrop and his company with the charter, the numbers of the colony had so much increased and their settlements had so expanded, that the natural result of a *representative* democracy, forced itself upon them. "Notice being sent out, " says Winthrop's Journal, (Savage's Winthrop, i. 128,) of the general court to be held the 14th day of the third month, called May, (1634) the freemen deputed two of each town to meet and consider of such matters as they were to take order in at the same general court; who having met, *desired a sight of the patent*, and conceiving thereby that all their laws should be made at the general court, repaired

to the governor to advise with him about it. He told them, that when the patent was granted, the number of free men was supposed to be (as in like corporations) so few, as they might well join in making laws; but now they were grown to so great a body, as it was not possible for them to make or execute laws, *but they must choose others for that purpose*; and that howsoever it would be necessary hereafter to have a *select* company to intend that work, yet for the present they were not furnished with a sufficient number of men qualified for such a business, neither could the *commonwealth* bear the loss of time of so many as must intend it. Yet this they might do at present, viz., they might, at the general court make an order, that once in the year, a certain number should be appointed (upon summons from the governor) to revise all laws and to reform what they found amiss therein; but not to make any new laws, but prefer their grievances to the court of assistants; and that no assessment should be laid upon the country without the consent of such a committee, nor any lands disposed of."

17 To the remark upon this passage of the last editor of Governor Winthrop's Journal, that no country on earth can afford the perfect history of any event more interesting to its own inhabitants than that which is here related, I will only add, that in this transaction, following as by the providential agency of a law of nature, the transfer of the charter of Massachusetts to this country, are to be found the *primordia rerum*[5], the first elements of that great, republican, democratic, confederated republic, destined to gather under the shadow of its wings, in its appointed time, perhaps the whole continents of North and South America.

18 The settlement of Connecticut was commenced in 1636 by Mr. Hooker with detachments from the inhabitants of Newtown, Dorchester, Watertown and Roxbury. They went out from the colony of Massachusetts and with some informal warrant from its magistrates, but their location was without the bounds of its charter. In 1631 , the Earl of Warwick had obtained from Charles the First, a grant of forty leagues of seacoast westward from the mouth of Narraganset river which had been assigned to Lord Say and Seal, Lord Brook and others, among whom were John Pym and John Hampden, and in 1635 a grant of sixty leagues of territory, including the Connecticut river, bad been made by the council at Plymouth to James, Marquis of Hamilton; but in 1638, on the 14th of January, the inhabitants of the towns of Hartford, Weathersfield and Windsor resorted to the

5 Literally translates to: the beginning of things.

usual expedient, of which the Plymouth pilgrims had set the first example, and formed among themselves a compact or consttution of government; "and well knowing where a people are gathered together, the word of God requires that to maintain the peace and union of such a people, there should be an orderly and decent government established according to God, to order and dispose of the affairs of the people at all seasons, as occasion should require," — they did therefore "associate and conjoin themselves to be as one public estate or commonwealth , and did for themselves and successors , and such as should be adjoined to them at any time thereafter, enter into combination and confederation together, to maintain and preserve the liberty and purity of the gospel of our Lord Jesus Christ, which they professed, and also the discipline of the church of Christ, according to the truth of said gospel as then preached among them; as also in civil affairs , to be guided and governed according to such laws, rules, orders and decrees as should be made, ordered, and decreed, as prescribed in the contract;" - that is, that two courts or assemblies should be held every year, at one of which election should be made of deputies and magistrates, and a governor to serve for a single year.

The colony of New Haven was settled by a company who came over 19
from England to Boston, in 1637.[6] Its most prominent members were Theophilus Eaton and Edward Hopkins, merchants of London, and John Davenport, a minister, who, says Neal, came over with a very great retinue of acquaintances and followers. They would have formed a precious acquisition of strength to the Massachusetts colony, the general court of which offered them a grant of any spot within their jurisdiction, upon which they could fix their choice. But the spirit of independence and self government, so transcendent over all others, among the Puritans of that age, and stimulated perhaps by personal aspirations of relative dignity, and consideration, in the bosoms of the leading laymen, or of their spiritual guide, prompted them. purposely to step beyond the jurisdiction of any charter, and to plant themselves in a valley where they might exercise the sovereignty of nature and establish a constitution of government founded on the solemnly settled principle that the holy Scriptures are the perfect rule of a commonwealth, and that the exercise of all the powers of government, should be exclusively committed to the members of the church. Such a government they did accordingly institute.

6 The colony of New Haven eventually merged with Connecticut.

20 These were the four colonies of New England united in the confederacy of 1643. The existence of four distinct communities of men, associated together, each by a separate primitive compact, settled on a territory so small as that of New England, and all consisting of one small religious sect of Christians, seceders from the church of England, may well lead an impartial observer of another age to conclude that if the spirit, under the impulse of which they all acted, was conscientious, it was also contentious - contentious far beyond the bounds of Christian charity. But there was yet another, a fifth New England colony, denied admission into the union, and furnishing, in its broadest latitude, the demonstration of that conscientious, contentious spirit, which so signally characterized the English Puritans of the 17th century, the founders of New England, of all the liberties of the British nation, and of the ultimate universal freedom of the race of man.

21 The founder of the colony of Rhode Island was Roger Williams, a man, who may be considered the very impersonation of this combined conscientious, contentious spirit. Born in the land of Sir Hugh Evans and Captain Fluellen, educated at the University of Oxford, at the very period, when the monarchical, episcopal church of England was purging herself as by fire from the corruptions of the despotic and soul - degrading church of Rome, he arrived at Boston in February, 1630, about half a year after the landing of the Massachusetts colony of Governor Winthrop. He was an eloquent preacher - stiff and self - confident in his opinions, ingenious, powerful and commanding in impressing them upon others, inflexible in his adherence to them, and by an inconsistency peculiar to religious enthusiasts, combining the most amiable and affectionate sympathies of the heart, with the most repulsive and inexorable exclusions of conciliation, compliance or intercourse with his adversaries in opinion. On his first arrival he went to Salem, and there soon made himself so acceptable by his preaching, that the people of Mr. Skelton's church invited him to settle with them as his colleague. But he had broached and made no hesitation in maintaining two opinions imminently dangerous to the very existence of the Massachusetts colony, and certainly not remarkable for that spirit of charity, or toleration, upon which he afterwards founded his own government, and which now, in after ages, constitutes his brightest title to renown. The first of these opinions was that the royal charter to the colony of Massachusetts was a nullity - because the king of England had no right to grant lands in foreign

countries which belonged of right to their native inhabitants. This opinion struck directly at all right of property held under the authority of the royal charter, and, followed to its logical conclusions, would have proved the utter impotence of the royal charter to confer powers of government any more than it could convey property in the soil.

The other opinion was that the church of Boston was criminal, for 22
having omitted to make a public declaration of repentance, for having held communion with the church of England, before their emigration; and upon that ground he had refused to join in communion with the church at Boston.

Other opinions, not less extreme, and shaking the foundations of 23
human society, were laid to his charge and were by him neither disproved nor disavowed. It cannot be surprising, therefore, that at that period the interference of Governor Winthrop and his assistants, by remonstrance or advice to the church of Salem, should have prevented his settlement there. He went to Plymouth and was soon settled in the church at that place. They had not the crime of communion with the church of England, before their emigration, to repent of in sackcloth and ashes; and they had no charter, the constitutional validity of which could be contested. But extreme opinions on principles of morals and radical abstraction affecting the origin and right of property are seldom solitary. Paradoxes are of a prolific breed, and Mr. Williams, popular as he always made himself in the pulpit, in the course of two or three years, held forth doctrines producing dissension and discord in his Plymouth flock, from which he solicited a dismission to the church of Salem, and it was granted.

Abstract truth, when coming into collision with human institutions, 24
and asserted with eloquent lips, never fails to make its way to the heart of man. In the interval of Williams's residence at Plymouth, Mr. Skelton had died, and his people, now in defiance of the remonstrances of the colonial magistrates, elected Williams for their teacher. His hostility to the foundations of the Massachusetts colony was neither confined to speculation nor merely defensive. It was altogether revolutionary. He denied utterly the validity of the colonial charter. He refused to take the oath of allegiance, and in retaliation of the remonstrances of the Massachusetts magistrates against his election, and of their withholding a grant of a lot of land, for which his church at Salem had petitioned, he prevailed on that church to write letters of admonition and "accusation" against the magistrates, to the

churches of which they were members. This, in the temper of the times, could be considered in no other light than instigation to rebellion. At the next general court, Salem was disfranchised till an apology should be made. This brought to a crisis the continued existence of the Massachusetts colonial government itself. The people of Salem submitted, apologized, and returned to their allegiance. The insurrection was subdued, tranquillity restored - all was quiet, "Præter atrocem animum Catonis."[7]

25 Williams had, by the subtlety and vehemence of his persuasive powers, prevailed upon Endicott to look upon the cross of St. George, in the banners of England, as a badge of idolatry, and to cause it actually to be cut out of the flag floating at the fort in Salem.[8] The red cross of St. George in the national banners of England, was a grievous and odious eyesore to multitudes, probably to a great majority of the Massachusetts colonists; but in the eyes of the government of the colony, it was the sacred badge of allegiance to the monarchy at home, already deeply jealous of the purposes and designs of the puritan colony. The charter itself was in imminent and daily danger of revocation, under the influence of Laud;[9] and nothing could be more clearly indicative of a spirit of total independence, than the exclusion of the cross from the colonial standard. At the next ensuing election, Endicott was left out of the magistracy, called to account before the general court, and sentenced as for a great offense - admonished and disabled for one year from bearing any public office; his judges declining any heavier sentence, because they were persuaded he did it out of tenderness of conscience, and not of any evil intent.

26 Mr. Williams, now in the further indulgence of his conscientious contention, required his church to break off from communion with all the

---

7 Translates to "Besides the terrible spirit of Cato." This is a line taken from poem 1 of book 2 of the *Odes* of Horace. The poem discusses the tragedy of the Roman civil wars. In the course of these wars, a great many of the respectable statesmen of the day surrendered to Caesar and thus acquiesced to his dictatorship. Only the radical stoic Cato the Younger committed suicide rather than dein to live under a tyrant.

8 Saint George is the patron saint of England and his cross is represented by the large red cross that forms the central part of the United Kingdom's national flag where it is joined by the Scottish cross of Saint Andrew and the Irish cross of Saint Patrick.

9 Adams is here referring to William Laud, who was appointed Archbishop of Canterbury by King Charles I and served as one of the chief advocates of Charles's more Catholic understanding of the Church. He was executed towards the end of the English Civil War. The religious movement Laudianism – which advocated high church ceremonies and clerical hierarchy – is named after him.

churches, not only of Old, but of New England. They were all unregenerate, and all communion of the regenerate with the unregenerate man was sin. His church staggered and paused. He gave them warning that if they would not separate from all contaminating communion with the unregenerate he would separate himself from them, and the deed followed the word. He opened a conventicle[10] in his own house, not unattended with followers, and quarreled with his wife for persevering to worship with that church which *he* had excommunicated as unregenerate. Can we blame the founders of the Massachusetts colony for banishing him from within their jurisdiction? In the annals of religious persecution, is there to be found a martyr more gently dealt with by those against whom he began the war of intolerance, whose authority he persisted, even after professions of penitence and submission, in defying, till deserted even by the wife of his bosom, and whose utmost severity of punishment upon him was only an order for his removal as a nuisance from among them. They would have sent him to England for a trial, far otherwise severe; but he escaped from their pursuit, and after wandering a winter long among the Indian savages, whom he had attached to him by his reverence for their rights, he attempted first to make a settlement at See konk, but finding that within the Plymouth jurisdiction, finally alighted at a spring at the head of a creek beyond all the chartered grasp of civilized man, and called it PROVIDENCE.

And here it was that he finally obtained, by means of grants of lands 27
from the Indians in that region, and in the neighboring island of Aquidneck, and lastly of a charter from the monarch of England, the occasion of establishing a colony upon his own darling principles of religious *toleration* and political *democracy*. From the moment they were delivered of his presence, there appears never in the Massachusetts colony the slightest disposition to persecute or molest him. It was by the advice of Governor Winthrop, given in a private letter, and encouraging him from the freeness of the place from English claims or patents, that he steered his course to the Narraganset Bay. Winslow, from the Plymouth colony, visited him, and put a piece of gold into the hands of his wife for their supply. And in the Pequot war of 1637 the English of Massachusetts employed him to make a league, offensive and defensive, with the Narraganset Indians, which he accomplished.

---

10 The term conventicle refers to a secret or illegal religious meeting.

28 The settlement of Roger Williams at Providence was made in 1636. The deed of the Sachems, Canonicus and Miantonomy, of his lands , was dated two years later, and contemporaneous with it to a day was their grant to William Coddington and his friends of the island of Aquidneck, afterwards, now, and for all future time known by the honorable name of Rhode Island. The joint government of which, under the form of a perfect modern democracy and by the name of the colony of Rhode Island and Providence Plantations, was first chartered by the usurped authority of the Long Parliament, then deeply tinged with aristocracy by a charter from the restored Stuart, Charles the Second, and recently, by a fearful political convulsion, reinvested by her own people in the attributes of democracy, modified by her more enlarged existence as a member of this great North American Union.

29 At the formation of the New England union, this colony solicited admission to the same, which was refused unless they would submit themselves to the jurisdiction of the Plymouth colony, which they declined. The union then consisted of four separate independent communities, in a great measure self-formed; the vital principle common to them all being religious contention — and the quickening spirit, equal rights, freedom of thought and action, and personal independence.

30 On the formation within our own times of the present North American confederacy, the commonwealth of Pennsylvania assumed, as the motto to her arms, the words, "Virtue, Liberty and Independence." Her neighboring sister, New York, under a prophetic transport, prouder if not more sublime, assumed, as the emblem of her futurity, with the image of the rising sun, the aspiring, solitary word, *Excelsior*.[11] Massachusetts, as if mindful of the whole history of her existence, from the tempest-tossed trials and dangers of the Mayflower pilgrims till the consummation of her own social compact in her state constitution, borrowed from Algernon Sidney the profound thought, that the only end worthy of the nature of man, of a struggle for liberty, is the enjoyment of peace and quiet, and taught her sons to be ever ready to draw the sword in her defence.[12]

---

11 A Latin phrase that means "ever upward."

12 The state motto of Massachusetts is "Ense Petit Placidam Sub Libertate Quietem," which translates to "By the Sword We Seek Peace, but Peace Only Under Liberty."

The New England confederation originated in the Plymouth colony and was probably suggested to them by the example which they had witnessed, and under which they had lived several years in the United Netherlands. Edmund Burke has called the puritan spirit the Protestantism of the protestant religion. Set aside the contentious element in the religious fervor of the Puritans, and you perceive no more adequate motive for Mr. Hooker and his little flock to seek an independent sub-sovereignty beyond the Massachusetts charter at Hartford, nor for Mr. Theophilus Eaton and Mr. Davenport to step again beyond the bounds of the Connecticut settlement to erect a new commonwealth at New Haven, than there was for Roger Williams to set up his standard of free thought and democracy at Providence. One colony would for all purposes, except that of religious controversy, have been amply sufficient to cover the whole surface of New England; and far more efficient for self-defence against the formidable and ferocious enemies by whom they were surrounded. For at the north they had to contend with the pretensions of a French settlement of Acadia, and at the west with that of Canada, under grant from the kings of France, while at the south, in the immediate vicinity of Connecticut river, the Dutch settlers of the Manhadoes were already contesting the possession of it with them. 31

The Plymouth pilgrims from the time of their landing, lived for years in peace and harmony with the neighboring Indians. The spot on which they built their town was, with regard to any right of occupancy or possession by the Indians, a derelict. It was found a perfect solitude. The first Indian chief who came among them, in March, after their landing, Samoset, told them, says the relation of Mourt, that the place where they lived was called Patuxet, and that, about four years before, all the inhabitants had died of an extraordinary plague; and there was neither man, woman nor child remaining; so that there was none to hinder their possession or lay claim to it. With the nearest neighboring chieftain or sachem they shortly afterwards had friendly intercourse, and formed a league of amity. This was Massasoit, the chieftain of Massachusetts, with whom they continued in friendship throughout his life, and from him received the grants of lands, as the borders of their settlements were enlarged. In the course of the first year of the colony, nine of the chiefs subordinate to Massasoit came in and acknowledged themselves to be the subjects of king James; but among them were at least some whose ideas of subjection were not very accurately 32 defined, or whose principles of good faith were not very deeply seated in their souls.

33 The Plymouth pilgrims had no ambition of conquest and no purpose of injustice to the natives of this hemisphere mingled up with their migration for settlement. But the seeds of jealousy, hatred and war between them had already been sown before their arrival. There had been for several years, transient intercourse between the two races by the occasional visitation and landing of trading adventurers, French as well as English, and scenes of fraud, violence and even bloodshed had embittered the passions of the Indians against the intruder upon his native soil. The country was besprinkled, it could not be said peopled, by scattered tribes almost always at war with one another. There were probably not thirty thousand of them dotting a surface of territory which at this day maintains a population exceeding two millions. Of their numerous tribes of smaller account, whose names have scarcely been preserved, there were, beside those ranging over the domain of Massasoit, three, ever arrayed in hostility for mutual destruction, and whose existence, and combinations, and oppositions, were equally portentous of destruction to the infant colonies from Europe - the Pequots, the Mohegans and the Narragansets.

34 The first exterminating conflict of the races was with the Pequots inhabiting that portion of Connecticut where now stands New London and along the borders of the Thames. The aggression and the first act of warfare came from them. The design of exterminating all the English settlements in New England was first conceived and matured by them.

35 In 1634 , the master and crew of a trading bark from Massachusetts had been treacherously murdered by men of this tribe on the Connecticut river. They averted war to avenge this act, by alleging that it had been in self defence, and by a deputation with presents and promises to deliver up the murderers. In 1637, after an abortive expedition under the command of Endicott, and the murder of John Oldham near Block Island, a joint force from Connecticut and Massachusetts, in one short campaign, by fire and sword exterminated the Pequot nation, leaving scarcely a solitary remnant of them to tell the tale.

36 Such was the result of the first war between the colonists of New England with the Indians, included within their borders. Its origin had been by the murder of individuals belonging to the Connecticut settlement. Its termination had been accomplished by the means of auxiliary force levied

by the principal colony of Massachusetts. One tribe was exterminated. But all the colonies were surrounded and intermingled with others between whom and their people, collisions of temper and of property were continually occurring, which threatened the existence of each of the separate colonies, and were daily maturing to a general conspiracy of the Indian tribes for the total destruction of all the colonies.

The course of events in the Pequot war, had brought home to the feel- 37
ings of the colonists, in the several establishments, the necessity of an organized union for the common defense, against their numerous enemies, civilized and savage. When the first expedition under Endicott was despatched from the Massachusetts colony in 1637, Winslow was sent from the governor and council of Plymouth to treat with them about joining in it. The obvious and urgent motives to the union, and the difficulties to be adjusted in its formation were then fully discussed there was mutual apology and explanation to account for the fact, that there had not been earlier movements towards united exertions to meet the emergency of the time. Winslow had been instructed to propose that the parties should engage to aid each other *in all their occasions*, & c., which was declined for the present, the government of Massachusetts preferring to reserve to themselves the right to judge the reasons of any such occasion as might fall out. They urged, how ever, immediate considerations to induce the Plymouth colony to furnish present aid, which the speedy conclusion of the war, however, rendered unnecessary, and as to the proffer of a permanent and general confederacy, they concluded to write further to them after the next general court.

The extermination of the Pequot tribe struck such terror over all other 38
Indian nations of New England, that several years passed away without further molestation from them. The region within the domain of Massasoit remained faithful to his engagements, and his followers never joined in any of the projects hostile to the colonial settlements. But the tribes in more immediate proximity to the Pequots, the Mohegans and the Narragansets, continued in a state of convulsive agitation. They had long been, with occasional intervals of quiet, at war with each other; there was a rancorous feeling of mutual hostility of long standing, always stimulating them to war. Uncas, sachem of the Mohegans, had attached himself warmly, and as faithfully as the fickle character of Indian fidelity would admit, to the interests of the English colonists, and Canonicus, sachem of the Narragansets, from motives of policy, as well as from impulses of a better nature, though

unable to preserve the peace between his tribe and the Mohegans, had, by concessions and submissions, averted the fatal enmity of the strangers from beyond the seas. His nephew, Miantonomy, repeatedly summoned to Boston to account for movements of ill - repressed hostility, and bound by acknowledgments of subjection and by stipulations of peace with the Mohegans, under the umpirage and guarantee of the colonists, finished by a sudden and treacherous attack upon Uncas, in which, however, he was defeated, taken prisoner, and put to death.

39 The confederation of the New England colonies was formed. The motives for its formation are thus explicitly declared in the preamble to the eleven articles of which it is composed. "Whereas we all came into these parts of America with one and the same end and aim, namely, to advance the kingdom of our Lord Jesus Christ, and to enjoy the liberties of the gospel in *purity*, with *peace*; and whereas, in our settling, (by the wise providence of God,) we are further dispersed upon the sea-coasts and rivers than was first intended, so that we cannot according to our desire, with convenience communicate in one gov ernment and jurisdiction; and whereas we live encompassed with people of several nations and strange languages, which may hereafter prove injurious to us and our posterity; and forasmuch as the natives have formerly committed sundry insolencies and outrages upon several plantations of the English, and have of late combined themselves against us; and seeing by reason of the sad distractions in England, which they have heard of, and by which they know we are hindered, both from that humble way of seeking advice and reaping those comfortable fruits of protection , which at other times we might well expect: We therefore do conceive it our bounden duty, without delay, to enter into a present *consociation*,[13] amongst ourselves, for our mutual help and strength in all our future concernments, that as *in nation and religion*, so in other respects we be and continue *one*, according to the tenor and true meaning of the ensuing articles. "1. Wherefore it is fully agreed and concluded by and between the parties or jurisdictions above - named, (Massachusetts, Plymouth, Connecticut and New Haven,) and they do jointly and severally by these presents agree and conclude that they all be and henceforth be called by the name of *the United Colonies of New England*."

---

13 An archaic word that refers to close fellowship between sometimes antagonistic groups.

And now comes the act of sovereign power. "2. The said United Colonies, for themselves, and their posterities do jointly and severally hereby enter into a firm and perpetual league of friendship and amity for offense and defense, mutual advice and succor upon all just occasions, both for preserving and propagating the truth, and liberties of the gospel, and for their own mutual safety and welfare." 40

The third article is a mutual guarantee to each *jurisdiction* of all the settlements within its own limits, with a stipulation against the admission of any other jurisdiction, or the union of any two of the jurisdictions in one without the consent of the rest. 41

The fourth provides that the charge of all *just* wars shall be borne in proportion to the *numbers* of male population from sixteen to sixty years of age, inhabitants of each jurisdiction. The commissioners for each jurisdiction were to bring in returns of their numbers and accounts of the charges of war, whether by service of men or otherwise - each jurisdiction or plantation to rate itself for the payment without the interference of the confederation, and the *advantage* of the war, whether in lands, goods or persons, were to be divided among the confederates in the same proportions. 42

The fifth stipulates the manner of claiming and obtaining aid by each jurisdiction, from the others, when invaded by any enemy whomsoever, upon the notice and request of any three magistrates of the invaded jurisdiction, the rest of the confederates were forthwith to send aid in the proportion of one hundred men for Massachusetts, to forty-five of each of the other confederates. The men to be armed and provided for the service and journey, by their own jurisdiction, and on their return, be victualled, and supplied with powder and shot, by the jurisdiction which sent for them. Each jurisdiction might furnish voluntary aid to its next neighbor in completing their respective quotas, and at the first meeting of to the commissioners, the cause of the war was to be duly considered, and if it appeared that the fault lay in the invaded jurisdiction or plantation, the whole charge of the war and of making satisfaction to the invaders, was to be borne by the wrong - doers themselves. 43

In the event of a threatened invasion, any three magistrates , or two, if there were no more in the jurisdiction, might summon a meeting of the commissioners at any convenient place, whence they might remove to any other place at their discretion, to consider and provide against the threatened danger. 44

45 The sixth article was the constitution of the commission, two members from each of the four jurisdictions: all in church fellowship, with full powers from their several general courts, respectively to *hear, examine, weigh*, and DETERMINE all affairs of war leagues, aids, charges, and numbers of men for war, division of spoils, or whatsoever is gotten by conquest, receiving of more confederates or plantations into combination with any of these confederates, and all things of like nature which are the proper concomitants, or consequences of such a confederation for amity, offense or defense, not intermeddling with the government of any of the jurisdictions, which by the third article is preserved entirely to themselves. The agreement of the eight commissioners, was sufficient for the carrying into execution any proposed measure; but the agreement of six required a reference to the four general courts"; the unanimous concurrence of which, was required for the prosecution of the measure by all the confederates. The commissioners were to meet once every year, the first Thursday in September, besides extraordinary meetings, according to the fifth article. The meetings to be held alternately, at Boston, Hartford, New Haven, and Plymouth , but twice in succession at Boston. Some middle place, convenient for all the jurisdictions, might be afterward substituted.

46 Article 7. The commissioners, or any six of them, were authorized at each meeting to choose from among themselves a President, whose office and work should be to take care and direct for order and a comely carrying on of all proceedings at the present meeting. But he had no power to hinder the propounding or progress of any business, or *to cast the scales*, otherwise than as above agreed.

47 The 8th article provides first that the commissioners shall endeavor to frame and establish agreements and orders in general cases of a civil nature, wherein all the plantations are interested for preserving peace amongst themselves and preventing (as much as might be) all occasions of war, or differences with others, as about the free and speedy passage of justice in each jurisdiction, to all the confederates equally as to their own; receiving those that remove from one plantation to another without due certificate; how all the jurisdictions might carry it towards the Indians that they neither grow insolent nor be injured without due satisfaction, lest war break in upon the confederates through such miscarriage. And secondly, there was a double provision for the delivery up of a fugitive servant upon the certificate of one magistrate, or other due proof; and of criminal fugitives from

justice, on the certificate of two magistrates. And if help should be required for the safe returning of any offender, it was to be granted to him that craved the same, he paying the charges thereof.

The 9th article cautiously guarded against the involvements of the confederacy in any hasty or inconsiderate wars, by a positive stipulation that neither of the four confederates should begin, undertake, or engage themselves or the confederation, or any part thereof (sudden exigents to be moderated as much as the case would permit, excepted) in any war whatsoever, without the consent of the commissioners, or of at least six of them. And no charge was to be required of any of the confederates in case of a defensive war, till the commissioners should have met and approved the justice of the war, and have agreed upon the sum of money to be levied, which was then to be paid by the several confederates according to the established proportion. 48

By the 10th article it was agreed that in extraordinary occasions, of meetings of commissioners summoned by the due number of magistrates, if any of the members of the commission should fail to attend, four of them should have power to direct a war which could not be delayed, and to send for due proportions of men out of each jurisdiction, as six might do if all were present -- but not less than six should determine the justice of the war or allow the demands or bills of charges or cause any levies to be made for the same. 49

And finally it was agreed that the confederacy should be perpetual and that if any of the confederates should break any of these articles, or be any other way injurious, to any one of the other jurisdictions, such breach of agreement or injury, should be duly considered and ordered by the commissioners, for the other jurisdictions, so that both peace and the confederation might be entirely preserved without violation. 50

In the analysis of this institution, we perceive first the exercise of sovereign power in its highest attributes . It is a league offensive and defensive between four separate communities, independent of each other, for the management of their common concerns, involving peace and war, and all those relations of intercourse in peace with other tribes or communities, in which the interest of all the confederates were concerned. Every other object of government was reserved exclusively to the separate jurisdictions. The distribution of power between the commissioners of the whole confederacy and the separate governments of the colonies was made upon 51 the same identical principles with those which gathered and united the thirteen English colonies, as the prelude to the revolution which severed them forever from their national connection with Great Britain. The New England Land confederacy of 1643 was the model and prototype of the North American confederacy of 1774. In neither of the two cases was the measure authorized or sanctioned by the charters of the several colonies parties to the compact. In both cases it was the great law of nature and of nature's God; the law of self - preservation and self-defense which invested the parties as separate communities, with power to pledge their mutual faith for the common defense and general welfare of all. The New England colonists, conscious of this self-assumed sovereignty, expressly allege the *sad distractions* of their mother country, depriving them of her protection, and encouraging their enemies to combine for their destruction, as concurring with the other causes to impose upon them the duty of rallying all their energies for their own defense. The North American colonies, for the same assumption of sovereign power, appealed to their chartered rights as Britons, and finding that appeal fruitless and vain, to their natural rights as men bestowed upon them by their Creator at their birth, and unextinguishable by human hands or human institutions.[14] The compact of the New England colonies, without the sanction of their sovereign, was yet not against him. The union of the North American colonies turned the artillery of sovereignty against the sovereign himself and demolished the throne of the oppressor with ordnance drawn from his own arsenals.

52 The first of the reasons assigned by the parties to the New England confederacy for their *consociation*, is the common purpose of their emigration from Europe and settlement in this hemisphere - to advance the kingdom of our Lord Jesus Christ, *and* to enjoy the liberties of the Gospel in *purity, with peace.* This purpose was two fold , and necessarily imported a system of national policy - the propagation of the Gospel bearing upon their relations with the aboriginal natives of the country and the enjoyment of their religious liberties, regulating their domestic relations among themselves, and their dependent condition on their sovereign and their country beyond the seas.

---

14 Adams is here referring to American colonists' initial attempt to claim their rights under the English Bill of Rights and the Magna Carta before turning to revolution and the broader principles of the Declaration of Independence.

Neither of these purposes formed any part of the motives for the North American union of 1774. The propagation of the Gospel in *New England*, had, in the interval of more than a century, been consummated, so far as it was consistent with the wise purposes of Divine Providence that it ever should be consummated, partly by the conversion, but far more by the extinction of the Indian race. In other and distant parts of our Union, we still continue to exterminate, under the semblance of civilizing and Christianizing the hapless remnants of the American hunters, of whom, within the compass of one more century, probably nothing will remain but a tradition. 53

The other object of the puritan pilgrims, in departing from the land of their nativity and their forefathers, to populate a wilderness, the free enjoyment of their religion, was fully and successfully accomplished before the occasion for the North American Union arose. Religion had ceased to be the cause or even the pretext for wars, between Christian nations, and the contentious spirit of metaphysical casuistry, no longer sharpened the discordant passions of man, when they turned to the primitive rights of man antecedent to all human association and to the harmonious adjustment of the rights of persons and of property granted by the God of nature, to his creature endowed with an immortal soul, perishable on earth, but destined to a purified nature and a more exalted world. 54

The New England confederacy was confined to the puritan emigration from England. Its elements were all homogeneous in their nature, and its professed design to continue them *one* in political organization, as they were in nation and religion, was of no difficult achievement. 55

Yet the New England confederacy was destined to a life of less than forty years' duration. Its history, like that of other confederacies, presents a record of incessant discord — of encroachments by the most powerful party upon the weaker members, and of disregard, by all the separate members, of the conclusions adopted by the whole body. Still the main purpose of the union was accomplished. The concerted organization of the Indian tribes was counteracted and defeated for the space of at least thirty years, during which period the united colonies had been growing in strength, which brought them triumphant out of the fiery ordeal of Philip's war. Nearly contemporaneous with that event was the dissolution of the New England union. In the progress towards that issue the condition of the parties to the confederacy had materially changed. The colony of New Haven had been 56 voluntarily merged with that of Connecticut - the high contracting parties had sunk one of their number. The commissioners were only six instead of eight, and for the last twenty years their meetings, instead of being annual, were held only once in three years. The final dissolution of the confederacy was effected by the tyranny of James the Second, in seizing and vacating the charter of the Massachusetts and Plymouth colonies; but even before that act it would seem that for six or seven years, not even the triennial meetings had been held. The last meeting of the commissioners, as appears in Mr. Hazard's excellent collection of their records, bears date in March 1678.

57 Of the North American confederacy, self-constituted in the progress of the revolution which converted the thirteen English colonies into independent states, New England forms a constituent part, at that time, perhaps, transcending in power and importance all the rest, but in the gradual lapse of time, by the relative rapidity in growth of other parts of the union, and especially by the accession of new members of different origin, now greatly reduced and daily declining in her influence as a component part of the union. She has, indeed, in a great degree, insensibly lost her distinctive character; divided into six separate states, and covering a surface of territory and an amount of population scarcely equal to that of the single state of New York, the connection of her States has no closer cement of institution or of intimacy than with the other states of the whole union. The intensely religious feelings and prejudices of her infancy have given way to universal toleration, and a liberality of doctrine bordering upon the other extreme of a faltering faith. New England, as a community, has, by her incorporation in the North American Union lost her distinctive character, and to a superficial observer, little remains of her but the name. As a portion of the great community of the North American Union, the unity and simplicity of her character, without being totally extinguished, have been transformed into one component part of a stupendous republican empire. An empire already bounded only by the Atlantic and Pacific Oceans, and, to the eye of prophetic inspiration, to be hereafter bounded only by the eternal ice of the northern and southern Pole.

58 My Brethren of the Massachusetts Historical Society, we have been told that it was a day-dream of our puritan forefathers, the first settlers of New England, that they were destined to be the founders of such an empire. The foundation upon which *they* held this edifice was to be erected, was the natural equality of mankind, and the two eternal pillars upon which it was

to stand were *civil* and *religious* liberty. The natural equality of mankind, a doctrine which they imbibed from the sacred fountain of the scriptures, taught in the history of the creation, and forming the foundation of the religion of Jesus, settled it forever that this empire must be that kingdom of Christ against which the gates of hell shall not prevail. For this foundation, the natural equality of mankind, and for these two pillars, civil and religious liberty, the North American Union, to whatever extent of dominion, and whatever succession of ages destined to endure, will be forever indebted to the puritan fathers of New England. Let our prayer ascend to Heaven, and our energies on earth be applied, to improve and perpetuate the blessings left by them as our inheritance

"To the last syllable of recorded time."[15]

---

15 This is a line taken from William Shakespeare's *Macbeth*. A broader expert of the speech delivered by Macbeth reads:

> "Tomorrow, and tomorrow, and tomorrow,
> Creeps in this petty pace from day to day,
> To the last syllable of recorded time;
> And all our yesterdays have lighted fools
> The way to dusty death. Out, out, brief candle!
> Life's but a walking shadow, a poor player,
> That struts and frets his hour upon the stage,
> And then is heard no more. It is a tale
> Told by an idiot, full of sound and fury,
> Signifying nothing."

Chapter 6: On the Haitian Revolution (1843)

On January 1, 1804, Haiti declared itself a free republic. Born of a slave rebellion that ended in the massacre of the formerly dominant white society on the island, the Haitian Revolution sent shockwaves through American society. Many Southern plantation owners feared that events in the Caribbean would repeat across the rolling farms of Dixie. As such, the nation of Haiti became a subject of deep political sensitivity – most mainstream politicians liked to avoid the issue so as not to upset Southern colleagues. This makes the short letter that closes out this volume all the more remarkable. Addressed to a community of Haitian immigrants in Maine, John Quincy Adams explained both the evils of slavery and expressed his belief in its ultimate extinction. Adams takes his letter one step further and lays at the feet of his country both the proclamation of mankind's universal equality but also the terrible evil of slavery.

1 I have received your letter of the 9th, and perhaps in answering it, my safest and most prudent course would be to express my regret, that the precarious state of my health, and particularly of my voice, would not warrant me in undertaking an engagement to deliver a public address upon any subject whatever, on the first day of next August. This answer I have been most reluctantly constrained to give to several other kind invitations to address the people on various subjects, in the course of the ensuing summer and autumn. But the occasion of which you propose to celebrate the anniversary, is viewed in lights so entirely different and opposite to each other that it cannot be denied to have assumed both a religious and a political aspect, and this must be my apology, while returning my thanks for your friendly invitation, for frankly unfolding to you other reasons which would have dictated to me the same conclusion, even if the state of my health admitted of my compliance with it.

2 The extinction of SLAVERY from the face of the earth, is a problem, moral, political, religious, which at this moment rocks the foundations of

human society throughout the regions of civilized man. It is, indeed, nothing more nor less than the consummation of the Christian religion. It is only as *immortal* beings that all mankind can in any sense be said to be born equal—and when the Declaration of Independence affirms as a self-evident truth, that all *men* are born equal, it is precisely the same as if the affirmation had been that all men are born with immortal souls. For take away from man his soul, the immortal spirit that is within him, and he would be a mere tamable beast of the field, and like others of his kind, would become the property of his tamer. Hence it is, too, that by the law of nature and of God, man can never be made the property of man. And herein consists the fallacy with which the holders of slaves often delude themselves, by assuming that the test of property is human law. The soul of one man cannot by human law be made the property of another. The owner of a slave is the owner of a living corpse; but he is not the owner of a man.

3 The natural equality of mankind, affirmed by the signers of the Declaration of Independence to be *held by them* as self-evident truth, was not so held by their enemies. It was not so held by the King and Parliament of Great Britain. They held the reverse. They held that sovereign power was unlimitable. That the tie of allegiance bound the subject to implicit obedience, and, therefore, that the natural equality of mankind was a fable. This was THE question of the American Revolutionary War. In the progress of that war, France, Spain, the United Netherlands became involved in it. The Governments of France and Spain, absolute monarchies, had no sympathies with the American cause—the rights of human nature. Vergennes had plotted with Gustavus of Sweden, the revolution in Sweden, from liberty to despotism.[1] Turgot, very shortly before the surrender of Burgoyne, but after our Declaration of Independence, had formally advised Louis the Sixteenth, that it was for the *interest* of France and Spain that the insurrection in the Anglo-American colonies should be *suppressed*.[2] France and Spain had been *warned* of the remote consequences to them as *owners of colonies*, of the success of the Anglo-Americans. But neither Turgot nor Vergennes, nor any one European or American statesman of that age, foresaw or imagined

1 Adams is here referring to Charles Gravier, comte de Vergennes, who as foreign minister of France collaborated with Gustave III of Sweden to end any vestige of republican government in that country.

2 Anne Robert Jacques Turgot, Baron de l'Aulne, was a French statesman and political theorist who served as first minister of state to King Louis XVI.

what would be the consequence, by no means remote, upon their own Governments at home, of the dismemberment of the British Empire, and the triumphant establishment, by a seven years' war on the continent of North America, of an Anglo-Saxon confederate nation, on the foundation of the natural equality of mankind, and the inalienable rights of man.

4 After Louis the Sixteenth lost his crown, he remembered, and bitterly repented the part he had taken on the side of the natural equality of mankind, and the rights of human nature in the American revolutionary war. For the revolution in France, by which he lost his throne and his life, was another fruit of the same self-evident truth, that all men are born equal, and have a RIGHT to life, liberty, and the pursuit of happiness, *without infringing* upon the same right of all other men.

5 Until the day of the Declaration of Independence, the condition of slavery was recognized as lawful in *all* the English colonies. The Constitution of the Commonwealth of Massachusetts, established three years after the Declaration of Independence, adopted its self-evident truths, and the Judges of the Supreme Court of the Commonwealth, under that Constitution, judicially decided that slavery within the Commonwealth was thereby *ipso facto* abolished. Since that day, there has not been a slave within the State.

6 The author of the Declaration of Independence was a slaveholder. His self-evident truths taught him that slave-holding was an outrage upon the natural rights of mankind, at least as great as Parliamentary taxation without representation. He held that opinion to his dying day. He introduced it into his draft of the Declaration of Independence itself, imputing the existence of slavery in Virginia, to George the Third, as one of the crimes which proved him to be a tyrant unfit to rule over a free people.

7 Among the signers of the Declaration of Independence, there were at least twenty slave-holders—or probably, thirty. They could not stomach the application of the self-evident truths to themselves, and they lopped it off as an unsightly excrescence upon the tree of Liberty. But his grandson and executor has carefully preserved it in the double form of print and facsimile, in the edition which he has published of his writings, and there it stands, an unanswerable testimonial to posterity. That in the roll of American Abolitionists, first and foremost after the name of George Washington, is that of *Thomas Jefferson.*

The result of the North American Revolutionary War had prepared the minds of the people of the British Islands, to contemplate with calm composure the new principle engrafted upon the association of the civilized race of man, the self-evident truth, the natural equality of mankind, and the rights of man. They had waged against it a cruel and disastrous war of seven years. Hundreds of thousands of valiant Britons had fallen victims, hundreds of millions of British treasure had been squandered to sustain the principle of illimitable sovereignty against the principle of illimitable human rights. The prize of the conflict was the liberty and the immortal soul of man. The contest was over between Britain and her children. The Lord of Hosts had decided the wager of battle. Human liberty was triumphant, and a new confederation entered upon the field of human affairs, with the Urim and Thummim of the Law from Sinai, "Light and Right," inscribed upon her bosom, and upon the diadem around her brow, "Holiness to the Lord." 8

But while this contest had been in progress, both of intellectual conflict and of mortal combat, the same question of human right against lawless power had been started in the land of both the combatants parties to this controversy. The question of the American Revolution had been of political government in the relations of sovereign and subject. Anthony Benezet, a native of France, settled in Pennsylvania, a member of the Society of Friends, and Granville Sharp, an English philanthropist, at London, were at the same time blowing the bugle horn of human liberty and the natural equality of mankind, against the institution of slavery practiced from time immemorial by all nations, ancient and modern.[3] There were two modes of slavery which had crept in upon the relations of mankind to one another, first as the results of war, by the right of conquest, and secondly, by the voluntary servitude of the feudal system. They had both become odious by the silent progress of Christianity. The practice of enslaving enemies taken in war had already ceased between Christian nations. The traffic in slaves had been denounced by the popular writers both of France and England—by Locke, Addison, and Sterne, as well as by Raynal, Rousseau, Montesquieu, and Voltaire. It was every where odious, but every where practiced, 9

3 Anthony Benezet was an American abolitionist and educator who lived from 1713 to 1784 and is often credited with founding the mainstream abolitionist movement. Granville Sharp was a British scholar who helped found the abolitionist movement in England; he lived from 1735 to 1813.

till just after the close of the American Revolutionary War arose the cry for the abolition of the African slave trade. The first assault of the Reformers was upon the trade which was prosecuted with such atrocious cruelty that the mere narrative of its ordinary details excited disgust and horror.

10 "Sweet are the uses of adversity," saith Shakespeare, and "in the day of adversity *consider*," saith yet higher authority.[4]

11 In the summer of 1783, when the results of the Revolutionary War presented themselves to the people of the British Islands, in the darkest form of adversity, they had, and they improved the opportunity, of considering the principle for which, and the principle against which they had so obstinately and fiercely contended. Their warfare had been against the self-evident truth of human rights. Thomas Clarkson, with two or three other Englishmen, associated themselves together with the purpose of arraying the power of the British Empire, for the total abolition of slavery throughout the earth; and the commission with which they went forth to regenerate the race of man, by leading captivity captive, was the same identical, self-evident truth against which Britain had just closed her relentless war, in humiliation and defeat. She was now to make the identical principle the inscription upon her banners—to war against *slavery* for the natural rights of mankind, and to proclaim the jubilee shout of liberty throughout the land—throughout the globe.

12 Of that undertaking, Clarkson himself has written the history. He has shown in what small beginnings it commenced, by what slow and almost imperceptible progress it advanced—by what interests, prejudices and passions, it was perpetually obstructed. How many years it was before it could obtain admission to the hall of legislation in the British House of Commons. How, in the meantime, it had been silently making its way to the hearts of the British people. How many struggles of argument and of eloquence it had to encounter, before it could lay prostrate all opposition at its feet—and how this emanation of the Christian faith, after waiting eighteen hundred years for its development, came down at last like a mighty flood, and is even now under the red cross of St. George, overflowing from the white cliffs of Albion, and sweeping the slave trade and slavery from the face of the terraqueous globe.

13 People of that renowned Island! Children of the land of our forefathers, proceed, proceed in this glorious career, till the whole earth shall be

4 A quote from William Shakespeare's *As You Like It.*

redeemed from the greatest curse that ever has afflicted the human race—proceed, until millions upon millions of your brethren of the human race restored to the rights with which they were endowed by your and their Creator, but of which they have been robbed by ruffians of their own race, shall send their choral shouts of redemption to the skies in blessings upon your names. Oh! with what pungent mortification and shame must I confess, that in the transcendent glories of that day, our names will not be associated with yours! May Heaven, in mercy, grant that we may be spared the deeper damnation of seeing our names recorded, not among the liberators, but with the oppressors of mankind.

Fellow citizens! The first impulse of the regeneration of human liberty 14
came from us—the Fourth of July is our anniversary day. Then was the principle proclaimed to the world as that which was to be the vital spark of our existence as a community among the nations of the earth. This is the brightness of our glory, and of this we cannot be bereaved. But how can we presume to share in the festivities and unite in songs of triumph of the first of August? Have we emancipated our slaves? Have we mulcted ourselves in a hundred millions of dollars, to persuade and prevail upon the man-stealer to relinquish his grasp upon his prey! Have we encompassed sea and land, and sounded the clarion of freedom to the four ends of Heaven, to break the chain of slavery in the four quarters of the earth? Has the unction of our eloquence moved the bowels of compassion of the holy pontiff of the Roman Catholic Church, to give his commands to his Christian flock against slavery and the slave trade? Have we softened the heart of the fiery Mussulman of Tunis, the follower of the war-denouncing prophet of Mecca, to proclaim liberty throughout his land?[5] Are *we* carrying into Hindustan the inexpressible blessings of emancipation?[6] Are we bursting open the everlasting gates, and overleaping the walls of China, to introduce into that benighted empire in one concentrated sunbeam, the light of civil and of Christian liberty? Oh no, my countrymen! No! nothing of all this. Instead of all this, are *we* not suffering our own hands to be manacled, and our own feet to be fettered with the chains of slavery? Is it not enough to be told that by a fraudulent perversion of language in the Constitution of the United States, we have falsified the Constitution itself, by admitting into both the Legislative and Executive departments of the Government,

5 Mussulman is an archaic word for Muslim.

6 Hindustan is an archaic word for India.

an overwhelming representation of one species of *property* to the exclusion of all others, and that the odious property in slaves?

15 Is it not enough, that by this exclusive privilege of property representation confined to one section of the country, an irresistible ascendancy in the action of the General Government has been secured, not indeed to that section, but to an oligarchy of slave-holders in that section—to the cruel oppression of the poor in that same section itself? Is it not enough that by the operation of this radical iniquity in the organization of the Government, an immense disproportion of all offices, from the highest to the lowest, civil, military, naval, Executive, and judicial, are held by slave-holders? Have we not seen the sacred right of petition totally suppressed for the people of the free States during a succession of years, and is it not yet inexorably suppressed? Have we not seen for the last twenty years, the Constitution and solemn treaties with foreign nations, trampled on by cruel oppression and lawless imprisonment of colored mariners in the Southern States? In cold-blooded defiance of a solemn adjudication by a Southern judge in the Circuit Court of the Union? And is this not enough?

16 Have not the people of the free States been required to renounce for their citizens the right of habeas corpus and trial by jury, and to coerce that base surrender of the only practical security to all personal rights, have not the slave-breeders, by State legislation, subjected to fine and imprisonment, the colored citizens of the free States, for merely coming within their jurisdiction? Have we not tamely submitted, for years, to the daily violation of the freedom of the post office and of the press, by a committee of seal-breakers: and have we not seen a sworn Post-Master General, formally avow, that though he could not license this cut-purse protection of the peculiar institutions, the perpetrators of this highway robbery must justify themselves by the plea of necessity? And has the pillory or the penitentiary been the reward of that Post-Master General? Have we not seen printing presses destroyed—halls erected for the promotion of human freedom leveled with the dust, and consumed by fire, and wanton, unprovoked murder perpetrated with impunity, by slave-mongers? Have we not seen human beings, made in the likeness of God, and endowed with immortal souls, burnt at the stake, not for their offenses, but for their color? Are not the journals of our Senate disgraced by resolutions calling for *war*, to indemnify the slave pirates of the Enterprise and the Creole, for the self-emancipation of their slaves, and to inflict vengeance, by a death of

torture, upon the heroic self-deliverance of Madison Washington? Have we not been fifteen years plotting rebellion against our neighbor Republic of Mexico, for abolishing slavery throughout all her provinces! Have we not aided and abetted one of her provinces in insurrection against her for that cause? And have we not invaded openly, and sword in hand, another of her provinces, and all to effect her dismemberment and to add ten more slave States to our confederacy?

Has the cry of war for the conquest of Mexico, for the expansion of 17
re-instituted slavery, for the robbery of priests, and the plunder of religious establishments, yet subsided? Have the pettifogging, hair-splitting, nonsensical, and yet inflammatory bickerings about the right of search, pandering to the thirst for revenge in France, panting for war, to prostrate the disputed title of her king, has the sound of this war-trumpet yet faded away upon our ears? Has the supreme and unparalleled absurdity of stipulating by treaty to keep a squadron of eighty guns for five years, without intermission, upon the coast of Africa, to suppress the African slave trade, and at the same time denying at the point of the bayonet, the right of that squadron to board or examine any slaver all but sinking under a cargo of victims, if she but hoist a foreign flag—has this diplomatic bone been yet picked clean? Or is our *indirect* participation in the African slave trade to be protected at whatever expense of blood and treasure? Is the Supreme Executive Chief of this Commonwealth yet to speak not for himself, but for her whole people, and pledge *them* to shoulder their muskets, and to endorse their knapsacks against the fanatical, non-resistant abolitionists, whenever the overseers may please to raise the bloody flag, with the swindling watchword of the UNION? Oh! my friends! I have not the heart to join in the festivity on the first of August, the British anniversary of disenthralled humanity, while all this, and infinitely more than I could tell—but that I would spare the blushes of my country—weigh down my spirits, with the uncertainty, sinking into my grave as I am, whether she is doomed to be numbered among the first liberators or the last oppressors of the race of immortal man.

Let the trodden-down African, restored by the cheering voice and 18
Christian hand of Britain, to his primitive right and condition of manhood, clap his hands and shout for joy on the anniversary of the first of August. Let the lordly Briton strip off much of his pride on other days of the year, and reserve it all for the pride of conscious beneficence on that day. What lover of classical learning can read the account in Livy or in Plutarch, of the

restoration to freedom of the Grecian cities by the Roman Consul Flaminius, without feeling his bosom heave and his blood flow cheerily in his veins? The heart leaps with sympathy when we read, that on the first proclamation by the herald, the immense assembled multitude in the tumult of astonishment and joy, could scarcely believe their own ears—that they called back the herald and made him repeat the proclamation, and then: "Tum ab certo jam gaudio tantus cum clamore plausus est ortus, totiesque repetitus, ut facile appareret, nihil omnium bonorum multitudini gratius quam libertatem esse. Then rang the welkin with long and redoubled shouts of exultation, clearly proving that of all the enjoyments accessible to the hearts of men, nothing is so delightful to them as Liberty." Upwards of two thousand years have revolved since that day, and the first of August is to the Briton of this age, what the day of the proclamation of Flaminius was to the ancient Roman. Yes—let them celebrate the first of August as the day to them of deliverance and of glory—and leave to us the pleasant employment of commenting upon their motives, of devising means to shelter the African slaver from their search, and of squandering millions to support on a pestilential coast a squadron of the stripes and stars, with instructions sooner to scuttle their ships than to molest the pirate slaver who shall make his flag-staff the herald of a lie.

19 Apologizing to you, gentlemen, for the length of this letter, I will close it with an ejaculation to Heaven, that *you* may live to substitute for the first of August, the day when *slavery* shall be proclaimed a word without a meaning in all the languages of the earth, and when the power of emancipation shall be extinguished in Universal Freedom. To share in the jubilant chorus of that day, if my voice could burst from the cerements of the tomb, it should be to shout Hallelujah! for the Lord God Omnipotent reigneth! let the earth rejoice and be glad!

John Quincy Adams

Index

Acknowledgments

This work would not have been possible without the generous financial support of the Institute for Humane Studies, the Bradley Foundation, and the University of Virginia's Karsh Institute of Democracy.

In addition, I would like to provide my deepest gratitude to the small team of research assistants who helped throughout the process of writing this book: Alayna Coleman and Ra'sor Woods.